GROWING UP
"UNACCEPTABLE":
HOW
KATHARINE HEPBURN
RESCUED ME

An Autobiographical Novel

Signe A. Dayhoff, Ph.D.

Growing Up "Unacceptable":
How Katharine Hepburn Rescued Me
By Signe A. Dayhoff, PhD

Copyright © 2015 by Signe A. Dayhoff, PhD
Published by Effectiveness-Plus Publications LLC
80 Paseo de San Antonio
Placitas, New Mexico 87043-8735

Depressed Girl with permission from Can Stock Photo
Katharine Hepburn in public domain via WikiMedia

Disclaimer: This book is sold with the understanding that the publisher is not engaged in rendering psychological or any other professional service. The instruction, ideas, and advice are not intended as a substitute for medical or psychological counseling. The reader should consult a professional to determine the nature of their problem. The author and publisher disclaim any responsibility or liability resulting from application of procedures presented or discussed in this book.

DEDICATION

This autobiographical novel is dedicated to all who have ever felt "unacceptable" at any time for any reason because of the perceptions, expectations, and/or actions of others. The sad young girl on the cover represents the child in all of us who has ever experienced emotional abuse and bullying from parents, siblings, other adults and children. It wasn't until I published this novel on Kindle that I discovered from hundreds who commented just how common this emotional abuse of children is in families. Also to my chagrin, I discovered that most families are indeed dysfunctional in the way that negative parental histories (both physical and emotional) play out in how parents deal with their children. Therefore, this memoir is also dedicated to all parents who unintentionally imposed their angst and emotional turmoil on their children. I hope this gives a little insight into their own pain as well as that of their children.

TABLE OF CONTENTS

CHAPTER 1   *"Meeting" Katharine Hepburn* 1

CHAPTER 2   *Bending Over Backwards to Please* 7

CHAPTER 3   *Cutting Out My Heart* 13

CHAPTER 4   *Sucking It Up Like a Good Little Soldier* 19

CHAPTER 5   *Impersonating His Desired Gender* 25

CHAPTER 6   *Drowning in Betrayal* 29

CHAPTER 7   *Outside Bullying* 36

CHAPTER 8   *Getting Extravagant Gifts* 39

CHAPTER 9   *Learning the Past* 44

CHAPTER 10   *Stability Spiraling Downward* 48

CHAPTER 11   *Confronting Polio* 53

CHAPTER 12   *Controlling Through Pain and Fear* 56

CHAPTER 13   *Marrying His "Evil Twin"* 62

CHAPTER 14   *Staking Her Claim Through Their Hearts* 70

CHAPTER 15   *Encountering More Valleys Than Peaks* 73

CHAPTER 16   *Embracing a Brief Encounter* 81

CHAPTER 17   *Still Expecting Change* 87

CHAPTER 18   *Mooching Off Relatives* 98

CHAPTER 19   *Bearing My Pre-Teens* 103

CHAPTER 20   *Embarrassing Me Publicly* 111

CHAPTER 21   *Stripping My Soul of Its Worth* 115

CHAPTER 22   *Rescuing My Mother* 120

CHAPTER 23   *Piling On More Humiliations* 124

CHAPTER 24   *Abandoning My Pets Again* 134

CHAPTER 25   *Leaving But Never Escaping* 138

CHAPTER 26   *Deciding Whose Pain is Justified* 143

CHAPTER 27   *Not Doing the Right Thing* 148

CHAPTER 29   *Risking Divorce* 159

CHAPTER 30   *Missing the Big Picture* 163

CHAPTER 31   *Forging a New Life* 165

CHAPTER 32   *Heading Back* 175

CHAPTER 33   *Binding Ties That Strangle* 181

CHAPTER 34   *Seeking Love, Deserving Pain* 186

CHAPTER 35   *Not Knowing What I Was* 191

CHAPTER 36   *Fearing Negative Evaluation* 193

CHAPTER 37   *Discovering the Roots of My Anxiety* 197

CHAPTER 38   *Forgiving My Father* 200

CHAPTER 39   *Empowering Myself!* 203

ABOUT THE AUTHOR..206

CHAPTER 1

"Meeting" Katharine Hepburn

Before the sledge hammer fell shattering my seven-year-old's world of warm, fuzzy assumptions about family and love, I was a relatively carefree second-grader, bright with a quick smile. I unquestioningly worshipped my "all-wise, all-knowing" father. This was, perhaps, even more than most children at that age because he was seldom around due to the requirements of his sales job. So when he was physically present, I tried to make the most of whatever time I had with him. I tried to show him how much I cared and seek his reciprocal feelings.

But one summer's day everything suddenly changed. As a result, I was thrust into what evolved into a two decades' long, conflict-ridden, wrenchingly painful personal struggle. It was a war between that voice in the back of my head that said I was "okay" and the powerful negative family circumstances that said I was anything but.

On that unforgettable day my father collapsed my house of cards with seven brief words. They started me on a downward spiral. I blamed and punished myself for not being "good enough to be loved." However, I simultaneously and incompatibly tried as hard as I could to find a way to make myself "acceptable" and accepted. The only thing I had going for me, to which I desperately clung for twenty years, was that small inner voice. It whispered encouragement to me. It stated in no uncertain terms why I was really "all right," in spite of everything that suggested the contrary. It indicated that I could survive. But in order to do it, I had to find a way to wholeheartedly *believe* in myself and then *act* on that belief ... despite my father's explicit condemnation of me.

That meant to my child's mind I somehow had to make my inner voice as real, concrete, and forceful as possible. That seemed the only way I could ultimately make myself into the acceptable person I felt I could possibly be. But how does a child do that? It felt like an insurmountable problem to resolve. I was confused, anxious, and desperate.

This was 1950 so there were no books or manuals on becoming your own person, especially for a female. This was the time when the culture was trying to get women back into the home to be homemakers and mothers after their having been independent workers in factory jobs for the war effort. I had no role models at hand from whom to learn anything like self-acceptance, self-esteem, and self-confidence.

The only place I could see women who appeared to see themselves that way was in the movies. It was there that female characters did not simply or easily accept criticism or humiliation from others. Instead, they stayed strong to do what they saw as important to them. So I slowly gravitated to the movies, both on the big screen and then on television. They would help me find out how I could make myself "okay."

But the wide range of disparate female characters in different situations was not going to be instructive enough for my purposes. What I needed was *one* character I could see repeatedly doing those things that spelled out inner strength. While female TV characters stayed in character repeatedly, they were all cast in the stereotype of being nurturing, not very bright, and secondary to men. That meant I would have to be find one movie character.

However, that too was a problem. Finding one female movie character being repeated in numbers of movies wasn't going to work either because they weren't. I'd have to find one actor, whom I could see more frequently as different characters who all tended to be strong. To be helpful she would have to represent and reinforce in bold letters the power and direction of that positive but wee voice in my head.

Over time I began to recognize that there was one particular actor who grabbed my attention. She seemed to be an especially illuminating and unremitting beacon of strength no matter what role

2

she took. She seemed to delineate a three-dimensional symbol of the tantalizing kick-butt possibilities for acceptability. She would become the person on whom I would to focus ...whom I would study. That was Katharine Hepburn. That realization sparked in me a tiny flame of hope. But, I would have to see her more often than I currently did in order to follow her actions. I hadn't the slightest notion how I'd do that.

Making myself "acceptable" would be no small feat. I was significantly hindered by my quest being vague and rationally unstructured. This meant I tended to go off on emotional tangents because my emotions were being allowed to take over. As I much later learned, before anything positive could happen I would have to determine not only what would make me "acceptable" but also how to accomplish it. Being so tied up emotionally at age seven, I would take twenty years to finally make my desired change a full and welcomed reality.

In the interim I personalized my inner voice and those positive yearnings as "my K.H." The more I watched Katharine Hepburn, the more outspoken she appeared to be. She refused to conform to societal expectations. That was an exciting possibility even at my young age. She could be vulnerable but also be as strong as Joe Louis's right hook and just as tough to handle. In movie news reels, she ran the gamut of emotions and behaviors to express and stand up for herself and pursue her goals. She opposed studios, campaigned for women's health gains, and fought against the Black List. She did what she felt was right.

I later learned her background supported my impressions of her screen and personal strengths. Because of a string of early box-office flops, her film career tanked. She was labeled "box office poison." But resilience was her middle name so she persisted, buying the rights to "Philadelphia Story," starring in it, making it a box-office smash hit. More flops, then "African Queen" which hit.

The cycle continued, but she never gave up, hitting again with "Long Day's Journey in to Night," and later "A Lion in Winter," to create an incredible sixty-year career. Her audiences loved her. She was a force to be reckoned with because she was, and still is even as a

3

legend, the embodiment of what we all strive to become: our own person, expressing it in our own way.

I initially divined my K.H. to help me decide not only how to get what I wanted but also how to feel good about myself for having accomplished what I had set out to do. To do this I fashioned my K.H. to be a paragon of virtues that I came to admire—such as, spirited, aggressive self-confidence.

My child's goal was to convince myself that through my practical K.H. I was destined to become my own person. This would be in whatever I chose to do no matter what I encountered. I would not permit anything to be an obstacle in my path. I would work persistently for what I sought, ever-assured I could achieve my objective ... in some way. That was a too-gigantic goal, but something I could aspire to in the beginning.

However, it was all-too-quickly apparent that my ideal of how I *should* think, feel, and act in furtherance of my goal was in total contradiction to what I actually did think, feel, and act at that time. While my mind wanted me to be my K.H. person, my tumultuous emotions compelled me to spend my time, energy, and effort to do *anything*, no matter how stupid or irrational, to get the love and respect I craved. I was possessed, needing to make myself feel whole.

A military-style conflict raged within me. Unfortunately, it was my emotional side that had all the heavy artillery and ammunition, rendering my rational side less well-equipped to fight this battle. As a result, I repeatedly spun my camouflaged vehicle's wheels. Sinking ever more deeply into the ruts of an ongoing muddy battle road, I opened myself to predictable pain and fear.

My K.H. was a peach-colored blossom on a desert prickly pear cactus, beautiful to behold to attract what she needed, but pointedly sharp to keep what interfered with her goal at arm's length. In contrast, I was a blushing little sweet pea flower, strangling myself with my own tendrils. Attempting to reach for the sun with one leaf, I held myself back with every geocentric movement of my roots. All the while, I was unaware of my self-destructive actions and either unwilling or unable to fight against them.

As a result, I did try to use Katharine Hepburn's film presentations, such as "Philadelphia Story," to get me thinking more

4

about how I could mimic her self-assuredness. In that film, she was a self-possessed heiress who forthrightly did what she considered in her best interest. Making lots of mistakes along the way, she always rose to the occasion with vigor and strength to correct those mistakes. But how would I extract those behaviors to make them my own?

There was an obstacle. There was no way I could see her as frequently as I deemed necessary to fulfill my obsessive desire to change myself in my father's mind. Moreover it would be a long time before VHS tapes and DVDs would be on the scene to allow repeated viewings of her film behaviors.

It wasn't long before I had to admit that my method of having only Katharine Hepburn's screen presentations available to emulate wasn't going to work right now. I couldn't pattern myself after her positive actions unless I saw her often. The only female I saw frequently was my mother, but she could not be my role model.

She had already begun to disappear into a pit of submissive anger and despair because of my father. Having been browbeaten for nine years by him, she was caught up in her own struggle, in the pursuit of her own circumscribed acceptance. She was in no psychological position to help me.

But, unbeknownst to me at the time, *she* was the one I was unconsciously observing. I was modeling myself after her. I was absorbing and acting on my mother's concrete behaviors and emotions. But those would all but guarantee my being treated like a door mat, like her. So despite my K.H. always murmuring positive messages in my ear, her rational words too often were drowned out by my desperate, unrequited yearnings to feel I belonged. They were too often stymied by my misdirected behaviors to achieve the unachievable.

This pitched battle between my rational and irrational side commenced with my having to walk this emotional tightrope which my father had strung for me across Niagara Falls. It swayed precariously in turbulent upper-loft winds and water spray, without a net below or my confidence to cross it safely. Even though my K.H. was quietly rooting me on, I stopped and remained frozen in the middle of the tightrope.

Nothing quelled my panic. I couldn't keep myself from looking down into what seemed like the misty abyss. I didn't yet understand emotionally it was truly possible to rise above these negative influences to express my K.H. I didn't yet acknowledge that I could cross the tightrope to then follow a yellow brick road to confident self-acceptance.

On this long journey I encountered a series of critical crossroads which I repeatedly handled badly. My fear grew and so did my irrational efforts to seek what I needed. While I was frantic to bring my K.H. to bear, I was also paralyzed by irrational inaction. There seemed no way I could get my father's acceptance as well as eradicate my insecurity.

As a child, my not handling the situations well was understandable. As an adult, my handling them disastrously indicated I was thoroughly hooked into destructive emotions and behaviors. Consequently, I spent years pushing a huge boulder out of my mental way only to later discover it was only an illusion. I was blindly flailing at windmills like Don Quixote.

Survival meant ultimately removing my irrational father from my head and replacing him with my rational K.H. And gradually my K.H. did help me break through that ten-inch-granite wall. It took seeing more of K.H.'s strong-willed-woman movies which grabbed my consciousness. They forced me to step back from my emotional addiction to see an indication of real-life options. In the end, I did discover that my unconditionally accepting myself was a far more important and realistic goal than my striving for anyone else's conditional acceptance of me.

What made my expedition out of my self-made hell possible was a query that perpetually played on my lips: "What would my K.H. do?" It helped me hang on to my submerged desire to confront and conquer my demons and establish my life. So what would my K.H. do on that particular August morning when the father I idolized revealed to me a secret that would unquestionably alter my life?

CHAPTER 2

Bending Over Backwards to Please

The heavy, sultry morning air was alive with the buzz of bees' wings as they flitted around the rose bushes, hollyhocks, delphiniums, and geraniums to fill the pollen baskets attached to their hind legs. They created a hum like that of a gigantic turbine set on "high" to power the sun. I thought if only their flapping could have also created a breeze to cool our over-heated, sweating bodies. Pudgy, with ear-length, mostly-straight medium blonde hair, I paused a moment to watch a bee snuggle into the heart of a pink hollyhock to relieve it of some of its honey-making gold.

My thirty-two-year-old father and I were in their midst as we strode across the rolling, carefully-manicured green lawn of Bowers County Club, located on the Pottsville Pike, outside Leesport, Pennsylvania. I had to double-time it because my stride was much shorter than my father's purposeful gait. We had just passed the regulation-size pool and skirted the large white beehive oven-extended bake house. This was where they baked their own bread, with the delicious, taste bud-tickling aroma that wafted toward our house when the winds were favorable. We were approaching the imposing white, columned country club building. It bordered the treed Schuylkill River creek, one hundred feet from us across the paved drive.

At the club its patrons could dine nightly *al fresco* on the lighted, breeze-cooled patio overlooking the sparkling, burbling water. Or, they could choose the more formal, smoke-filled inside dining room, decorated in white with a coffered ceiling, ornate moldings, and paintings of the gentry riding to the hounds. We had never eaten there but I had checked it out from the patio, peering inside through its French doors, when we were given the grand tour by the owner.

The large, industrial kitchen was stationed below. Meals were transported by large dumbwaiters to the floor above for not-so-dumb waiters to collect and serve. Hoisting myself up and down by the rope cables of the dumbwaiter was something I dreamed of doing, after having seen it in a movie.

I wondered what other services the "country club" provided besides food, drink, and access to the pool. There was no golf course, horseback riding, or boating. Fishing was poor pickings, limited to small sun fish in the shallow creek waters. It was there with undisguised disgust that I baited hooks with live worms for my father. He said the worm didn't feel it but I wasn't the least bit convinced. It was alive, responded to pain, and I wanted no part of it.

It was on this imposing property that we rented the caretaker's cottage. Constructed of river stone, this two-story, three bedroom house was across a gravel road from their large, pine-studded game preserve. The gravel road from some unknown destination ran past the house to meet the drive, main road, and entrance to the club parking lot. I wanted to walk up that gravel road to see where it went but never really did. I always let myself be distracted by different flowering plants along the way, like Queen Anne's Lace which butterflies liked.

Since we had no garage available, we had to park on the paved road just to the right of where the gravel road began. With the car exposed to Pennsylvania's icy, snowy winters, I was forever chipping seasonal accumulation off the windshield. I tried not to gouge the frozen rubber of the windshield wipers of our late-1940's black Chevrolet. But my being short created a distinct disadvantage to my doing it properly.

My father and I were heading back to the house after having released our three horses, Princess, Crackers, and Red, from the eight-stall red barn for their daily exercise routine. They would spend several hours in the white-fenced corral running freely and playing before we saddled and rode them. I had filled their large steel, half oil drum-like water trough, which was supported by a cross-beam wood cradle, with the green hose that snaked from the spigot outside the barn. As I did that, my father hauled a twine-secured bale of hay from the storage area beyond the stalls out to them.

Often it was my job to haul the heavy, unwieldy bale. I spent a lot of time jockeying the bale so as not to drag it through the dirt in the footfall-created path to the corral. On end the bale was my height. In the summer the sweet-smelling hay shafts stuck me, gluing themselves to my sweaty arms, haltered chest, and bare legs, making me itch and sneeze.

The other side of the corral was a long, windowed chicken house which ran the length of the oblong horse enclosure. Because of the sawdust on the floor, discarded feathers, and their grainy foodstuffs, one really should have a mask and respirator, even with the windows open, in order to see and breathe in there. It made me sneeze repeatedly. I felt sorry for the chickens having to inhale the dust and the fumes from their own nitrogenous waste in this hot building. They supplied the country club with fresh eggs and chicken flesh for all sorts of fancy menu items. I didn't like to think about their being slaughtered.

Beyond the corral and chicken house was a low-lying, maple-treed picnic area, with three redwood tables and benches and a large gazebo. The area was frequently flooded in the late-winter and early-spring by the creek beside it overflowing its banks. One winter the resulting pond froze. To my amazement my mother still had her Norwegian father's black racing skates. So I filled them with rolled up socks to try my hand at impersonating Norwegian three-time-Olympic figure-skating champion Sonja Henie. Falling numerous times, I did accomplish one upright, three-foot glide, before falling again.

It was a freeing experience. I felt as if I could be on my way to athletic prowess and renown if I wanted ... if I had more practice. I had a secret list of heroines I wanted to be like. They represented all areas of endeavor from painter Georgia O'Keeffe to ballerina Anna Pavlova to blues singer Ella Fitzgerald. My mother told me not to share it with anyone—but most especially not with my father.

At the other end of the corral, closer to the pool, was a pump house backed by six-foot-tall climbing rose bush. In its higher branches among the pale pink single-petal blossoms with yellow stamens was a ten-inch diameter spider's web of perfect geometric construction. In the center of the diaphanous net was a large yellow and black garden spider. Its eight legs were stretched out full from its body as if it were basking in the sun, warming up its interior after having been coated with morning dew.

My father continued walking as I paused to take in the delicate Irish-lace handiwork of the web. I marveled at such a beautiful insect being so skilled. Spiders, like snakes, always fascinated me so I was careful not to harm them if possible, unlike mosquitoes and flies which met their doom with a vengeance as soon as they approached me. A born rescuer, I saved all kinds of animals, including snakes, from danger on more than one occasion. This included a three-foot-long rattler. It had gotten caught in chicken wire surrounding our caretaker's cottage flower garden the week before. A great hunter, its mouse-filled belly rendered it too big to ease through the wire. It was securely trapped.

When I discovered it, I ran to my father's tool box in the conservatory/storage room in the back of the house. Its front half was in among the marigolds while its back half was still in the grass outside. Stuck, it flicked its tongue to catch scents on the air, like my presence. With one gloved hand just behind its head holding it down, I used wire cutters in the other to carefully cut away an opening around its bulging abdomen. Its tail rattled but only briefly.

Just as I finished, I quickly stepped back over the wire, let go of its head, and gave its tail a small poke. The snake slithered through without a scratch. It never looked back. That felt good. Its eating the mice that tried to enter the house was thanks enough.

My father, J.W., worked as a traveling salesperson for the Parker Pen Company, out of Janesville, Wisconsin. Selling to pen, jewelry, and department stores, he covered the whole of eastern Pennsylvania. It was a large territory. When he was at home, I was always occupied with trying to impress him with my having developed some form of "perfection."

Perfection was something he admired in all endeavors. However, it made my being his child problematic because I was good but I wasn't "perfect." I made lots of mistakes and ... as a result, was quickly apprised of them all as they each occurred.

Despite my efforts, it was clear that my father's interest was focused primarily on my brother, Wally (J.W. the Third). He was four years my junior and often seemed to me to be able to do no wrong in my father's eyes. Toe-headed with heavy-lidded blue eyes and an infectious smile, he was gangly and gawky, always eager to please his dad with a game of catch.

Being achievement-oriented, I used this sibling rivalry to spur me on to try even harder to gain my father's attention. Still he didn't want to play catch with me, saying, "Girls don't play catch." That wasn't true. I knew I could do it. I may have been a little overweight, but I was athletic and up for anything having to do with sports, games, and fun, especially with my father. Taking nothing for granted, I continued to pursue my overall goal of his attention with perseverance.

There had been another brother, J.W. the Second, who came two years after me. He died in infancy of SIDS (sudden infant death syndrome). He too was blond and blue-eyed, with chubby pink cheeks, grabbing sweetly at my mother in his own uncoordinated fashion as she rocked him in her chintz-covered rocking chair. His death was so traumatic for my father that I later wondered if a large part of him had ceased to breathe too. If that part of him had never fully recovered from it, having shriveled up, and died.

At the time he seemed to treat my mother as if she had personally suffocated *his* baby boy. He didn't speak to her, ignored her except when he had to communicate with her. I didn't know what it all meant. It worried me no end. Could he just reject people like that and treat them as if they didn't exist? If he could do it to her, could he do it to me? Later, it seemed to me he had retreated within himself, grieving imperceptibly, leaving my mother all on her own.

As a result, my mother seemed to spend a lot of time off somewhere else, maybe thinking. Later on, I suspected she had relegated her own grief to lonely contemplation wrapped in a silken cocoon of guilt. She appeared to ceaselessly ponder if maybe she could have ... should have ... been able to detect something was amiss in time to change the outcome.

While she sank into self-recriminations, my father seemed to ferment his sense of loss in anger, continuing to stew in this toxic

11

liquid even afterward. I was confused. I felt alone as my parents each went off to their private inner spaces. Then Wally was born to take his brother's place.

CHAPTER 3

Cutting Out My Heart

We were nearly to our house which was shrouded by two forty-foot catalpa trees with their large heart-shaped, leathery leaves. They carelessly littered the small front yard of grass. First it was with their large blossoms that turned rank as they quickly decayed and second it was with their five-inch-long brown seed pods. It was a hard-to-rake-up mess; I had the raking chore. The house featured welcoming French doors in the living room which opened onto a wide, columned concrete front porch painted white with two steps to the flagstone walkway down to the paved road.

One time as I sat on those steps, wondering where our two dogs had run off to, a large swallowtail butterfly gracefully glided toward me and alighted on the index finger of my right hand. I was so thrilled. I didn't dare move. Barely breathing, I didn't want to disturb it. I dearly wanted to stroke its velvety, black striped yellow wings but worried I might damage them if I did. Their wings were supposed to have powder on them that protected them. Touching would displace the powder and leave their wings vulnerable. I did not want to harm it.

Instead, I cautiously, gently stroked its black shell-like back. I couldn't swear to it, but I think the butterfly enjoyed my touch. Its long, wiry black antennae twitched and it seemed to unroll its black proboscis. It was so incredibly delicate and life-affirming. I so wished it would come back to me again and again to repeatedly share this moment.

I'd heard that some people raised butterflies. That sounded heavenly, being able to watch them come into being and then releasing them to add to the beauty of the world. But my butterfly soon lifted off and fluttered silently away. I gazed after it, still immersed in the Zen-like instant. There was no way I could at seven years describe what being in and with Nature meant to me. Except to say, I sensed it filled my soul in a way humans didn't.

As we approached the gravel driveway and our walkway, my father suddenly stopped. He turned to me with a serious look on his face. His dark brown hair was wet and lank with sweat and fell onto his flushed, furrowed brow. I stood at-attention, as ramrod straight as I could muster, listening hard, awaiting any pearls that might drop from his lips.

I always hoped that whatever he said to me would be something special that he wanted to share with me ... and me alone. Possibly it would be something nice about me ... something which I yearned to hear but seldom did. He was not generous with compliments. But that made them that much more valuable when he did share them.

As I waited in rapt anticipation, I took a deep breath, still breathing hard from having tried to keep up with him. He was going to confide in me, I knew it. Finally he was acknowledging me as mature enough at seven to be the recipient of his thoughts and feelings. How long I had waited for this moment. My heart started to pound and I shifted from one foot to the other. I'm ready. I wanted to flash at him like a neon light to let him know ... so hurry up. The suspense was killing me.

But then my expectations stopped cold. There was a hint of something akin to regret shadowing his dark features. It was a just-noticeable-difference in his countenance that my still-developing social radar could detect. He leaned over, his hazel eyes fixed on my cheek. Avoiding my eyes, he solemnly said, "I wanted a boy instead of you."

I ceased breathing. What? I didn't understand. Shock enveloped me. It was like a wet plaster of Paris death mask suffocating me. I stood there, my mouth agape, uncomprehending. My brain felt stuffed with cotton wadding. Had I heard him ... correctly? What did he say about a "boy instead"? What was it supposed to mean to me? My mind was reeling.

If I had been older, I could have stood back from it. It would have been obvious to me. He was saying, in essence, *In case you hadn't already guessed, you're a disappointment to me. You're not what I bargained on. I threw the dice and you came up craps. I didn't want you. You're old enough now to know you are not acceptable to me because you're a "girl, not a boy." Life's a bitch, but there it is. Deal with it.*

But as a little kid, I couldn't stand back. I was just getting a handle on abstract thinking and knowing that there was a K.H. available to me. I didn't yet have the cognitive facility to manipulate this concept. I couldn't look at all its dimensions from different perspectives to see how it could be made into something understandable. My "what?" quickly faded into my "why?"

Panic clutched my throat and tightened. My heart was galloping now. I must have done something terribly wrong. Hardly able to put two thoughts together, I strained to scour my memory. My brain had iced over. Crystals pierced and shut down all dendrites, axons, and synapses. Nothing useful could come to mind.

What had I done? I *must* have done something terribly, horribly wrong. But what? I was grasping at straws. Wally and I hadn't had any fights lately. I stayed away from the country club pool when I was alone. I hadn't wandered off by myself anywhere. I stayed away from the game preserve. I walked the dogs as directed. Thoughts unwrapped haltingly like a roll of cling wrap.

Or maybe it was something I hadn't done that I should have done? Let me ... let me think. Did I forget to muck the stalls for the horses? Or put down straw for bedding? Or fill their individual water buckets? Or give them hay and molasses oats? No. Had I sassed my mother? Not helped with the dishes? Not made my bed? Not done what little homework I had in second grade? Or not jumped to attention quickly enough for my father?

No, I ... I didn't think so. But wouldn't someone have told me if I had been skating on melting ice before I fell through and was flailing about, attempting to keep my head above the heat-sapping water? Could I have done something so un-recoverably bad that I deserved "not being wanted" as my punishment?

15

I immediately recalled having unknowingly skated on thin ice before. When I was much younger, my mother was helping bathe me in the bath tub. She had said, "It's time to get out of the tub now," and I responded to her, "No," as I continued to sit in the waist-high water, facing her, smiling, splashing, enjoying myself. I hadn't yet recognized that she easily and quickly took offense at whatever she perceived to be disobedience.

Slapping me hard across the face, she sent my head whipping to the right and knocked out a tooth that had been waiting to leave my mouth in exchange for a nickel from the Tooth Fairy. With her right hand still raised as if to lash out at me again, she shouted with a malevolent fury, "Don't you *dare* ever sass me again! Do you hear me? DO YOU HEAR ME?!" I was shocked, stunned. I nodded, "yes." My hand rushed to my left cheek as if to comfort it and protect it from further assault. Why? Why did you do that? What did this mean? Are you going to hurt me ... again? Mommy, don't hurt me. I'm sorry.

Her striking me in the face was appalling to me in more ways than one. It stung, leaving her fingers imprinted in red on my small cheek. But it also seemed a too intimately hurtful form of retaliation for a mother to give to her young child. I would never—could never—forget it. I quickly learned that saying "no" was a very dangerous thing to do with both my parents. Later on I tried to think of her action as understandable. But no matter how I tried to excuse it, it didn't pardon what felt like her communicating to me, "I hate you."

At the time it worried me no end. I was confused about what it meant for our relationship. Did that mean she didn't love me? Was I so unlovable? I'd have to be super-careful what I said to her from then on out. I wasn't sure I knew what all constituted "sassing" for her. Was it just saying "no"? Or was it something more? How would I know? Would I have to just risk it, hoping for the best? One thing it did was to make me sure my mother would tell me, then and there, verbally *or* nonverbally (or both), if I had done something to displease her. She definitely would not hide it for long.

I wanted a boy instead of you. My little gray brain cells couldn't quite stretch themselves around this statement. From what my evolving analytical faculties could determine, he was saying he didn't want *me* specifically. No. No, I did *not* want to think that. That was

16

too threatening. Mentally shaking my head to shift the pieces of puzzle into place, I tried to hang on to the notion that it must have been because of some unacceptable behavior.

I never said a word but asked in my mind: What did I do? Tell me what it was. I can do better; I know I can. I won't do it again, I promise. Just give another chance. Please! Just tell me what it was. Please? No matter how I tried to persuade myself it wasn't true, it was clear I was being rejected. But why was this happening? How could he feel this way? I'm your daughter, aren't I? I'm your child. You're supposed to love me, aren't you? You can't just reject me, can you?

My newly-acknowledged K.H. was stealthily invading my consciousness. Awareness was slowly coalescing into a solid sense that it really was about me as a person. And strangely, it had to do with the *sex* I happened to have been born with. What? That didn't make any sense to me. Wasn't my being a girl okay? No ... apparently not.

The pain started. It was as if my father had begun dripping acid slowly onto my skull, flaying off the skin, corroding the bone, drilling a hole into my brain's surface, burning away every thought and emotion of security and belonging.

Like standing at the bottom of a dark cavern of bewilderment and fear, I tried to get my bearings and make sense of it all. But the blackness was overwhelming. The only thing that was crystal clear was that I had just been excommunicated from the only family I had ever known. They were the ones about whom I cared and who I *had* thought loved me. But now I no longer truly belonged ... because I was "unacceptable." I was something worthless, to be tossed away because I wasn't a boy. I felt two inches tall and fading quickly into invisibility.

Ironically, what my father had said to me was definitely something for my ears alone. He had shared himself with me as he had never before and would never again. He had revealed thoughts both serious and devastating. But in doing so, he had sunk vampire fangs into my neck and was draining my life's blood.

It was my first in-your-face warning that I couldn't always trust and count on those close to me for support and caring. Even though I was naturally compelled to seek out love and support, I would have to be very careful where I did it. There are unexpected dangers lurking. And ... there is no way I could know ahead of time what specifically I could do ... or be ... that would get me rejected.

My synapses were setting off a chain-reaction of neuronal fireworks. Thoughts gushed and tumbled upon one another. I wondered why he was telling me this. What does he want me to do about it? Was I supposed to pack up my belongings in a red-and-white bandana, attach it to a stick, and leave home to hop a freight train like a Woody Guthrie or become a hobo living in a shack? Was I supposed to become some vague resemblance of a boy that he really wanted? But I wasn't a boy! If I did that, would that make him love me then? Even at seven years old I knew I wasn't going back to the womb to be part of some *in vitro* chromosome-exchange program so he could get the model he really wanted.

The sixty-four thousand dollar question was: How am I supposed to respond when the person I want most in the world to care about me tells me to forget it? Hot tears stung my eyes but I clenched my teeth—teeth which later in my life would be ground down to stubs from my years of clenching. This ongoing stress habit would later create TMJ (temporo-mandibular joint disorder) and require extensive and expensive dental work to produce a mouthful of crowns ... as well as the ongoing use of a dental appliance to prevent further flattened, cracked, and broken enamel.

Over the years I found I had developed lots of subconscious ways to punish myself for being pinned with the scarlet "U" of "unlovable" and "unacceptable."

Responding to my father, my K.H. would not cry. Instead, she would set her jaw and plow ahead. So I vowed not to shed one tear. Besides, would a boy cry? No. Boys weren't supposed to cry. Maybe since I couldn't actually *be* a real boy for my father, I could at least act like one. Maybe I could be a stalwart little soldier and suck it up. Maybe, if I did it right, he'd love me ... at least respect me for my efforts to give him "something" of what he so desperately wanted.

CHAPTER 4

Sucking It Up Like a Good Little Soldier

Still rendered insensible and not fully appreciating the consequences and implications of my father's heart-piercing words, I needed to tell someone. I needed to tell my mother what had happened. I wanted to tell her that I felt betrayed and abandoned. I needed her to comfort me, support me, and say I was okay.

It peripherally occurred to me that my mother might conceivably share his disappointment in me and regret my birth. But that wasn't how she related to me in general. My enthusiasm about sharing with her evaporated quickly as I considered what exactly I could say to her ... and how she might respond with her quick-to-anger temperament.

He hadn't said he was disowning me or dropping me off at the nearest orphanage or tossing me into a burlap bag to drown me like an unwanted kitten in the creek. What twisted my heart was mostly a feeling of disillusionment, emptiness, and fear. I had been rendered valueless and imperceptible.

More importantly, my telling her, speaking those soul-killing words out loud, would make it all too real. Right now it was only like a dark polarized electrical cloud had invaded and overhung my mind, zapping me with sparks of "what ifs." Maybe, I wished hard, it was really only a bad daydream or a heat-induced delusion. But I knew better. It engendered a shiver of terror down my spine.

My nose began to tickle as my eyes filled again and I swallowed hard. But what if she agreed with my father? Yes, she was much more caring than he. She read to me every night, especially L. Frank Baum's *Wizard of Oz* series. She tenderly cared for me when I had repetitive episodes of strep throat, mastoid-bone-related ear infections, and tonsillitis. But I saw it was wearing on her because I was sick a lot. She also demonstrated that she was unhappy with her lonely lot in life and with my father. It was obvious this was not what she had planned on in more ways than one.

Perhaps not surprisingly, many years later she did admit to me she never wanted children ... but, added she was glad she had me. That "but" always sounded to me like an after-thought. It came when she was ill and I was running myself ragged caring for her for the three years before her death. It made me wonder *when* she had decided that I was "all right" after all.

As a child, I had always tried to be her friend since she was so isolated out in the hinterlands by herself. Maybe she didn't feel that she counted either. But even feeling that, she couldn't ... she wouldn't ... dismiss me too, would she? I was worried and it constantly gnawed at me, creating stomach pains which I didn't dare complain about.

The reality was that my father ruled autocratically. As a result, my mother was becoming more and more subservient to him while becoming increasingly angry about it. He seemed to rarely give her much credit for what she did, said, or thought. When he spoke to her, he seemed to criticize her opinions and the things she did. He even often made fun of her singing to herself: that she substituted "dah-dah" for the words she didn't know, got some words wrong, or wasn't in perfect pitch.

My lingering impression was one of his unkindness and distance toward her which had started small but grew over time. In his sense of "personal perfection" he seemed to see himself as the ultimate judge of everyone else's behavior. Sometimes my mother would put her arm around my shoulders for no apparent reason. When that happened, I rejoiced at her touch and could smell her Tabu perfume which always enveloped me in the warmth of what I imagined as love.

But at other times she seemed distant from me. It made me wonder if she felt I were in the way or another problem with which she had to constantly deal. Would she defend me to him? Or would she protect her seemingly tenuous position and agree with him?

My K.H. indicated she would play it safe considering the risk of not doing so. I decided that I couldn't take the chance of her removing her support from me too. Her perceived support now would be the only thing keeping me afloat, connected, and "belonging" in some sense. I had to belong somewhere somehow.

Instead of breaking down in front of my father, I choked everything down and began to fashion a new goal for myself. I put it into action immediately. I resolved I would work even harder to do everything I could think of to make him accept me ... as a "boy." It seemed like a peculiarly counterintuitive thing to do but I saw no other alternative. I felt compelled to do *something*. He could abandon me but I couldn't abandon him. We were still joined emotionally at my heart as far as I was concerned.

As a result, I dressed with white tank tops and shorts. I swaggered when I walked. I pitched my voice lower. I even went hunting crows with my father. I hated how I was behaving, sacrificing myself for him. He'd have to appreciate that I was doing anything—everything— I could to give him what he wanted to make him happy.

His interest in "hunting" was very problematic for me. I loved animals and refused to hurt them in any way. Why did he want to shoot and kill crows, or anything else for that matter? That made no sense to me. He ostensibly loved animals, always having wanted to be a veterinarian to help them. How do you kill what you love? To me that was black and white.

It was in this area I quickly discovered I could take my boy-pretense only so far. Feeling tormented about the possibility of harming animals, particularly as "sport," I knew I had to break rank. I had to step out of this new "masculine" role... no matter what it might cost me. "Boys," so far as I could tell, were supposed to, expected to, or maybe positively sanctioned to kill things and think it was okay, weren't they? I didn't see how they could.

Animals made my existence worthwhile. They were honest. They appreciated my caring attention and showed me their gratitude. They listened to me. I could tell them *anything* and they wouldn't laugh or criticize me or break my confidence. They didn't think I was chubby or stupid. They physically touched me and allowed me to touch them back to make a warm, loving connection. They never hurt me purposely. I respected them. They respected me in return. But, perhaps, most importantly, they accepted me without judgment ... without conditions. And ... they *never* betrayed or abandoned me.

Animals shared the earth with us, often preceding us here. They deserved to live on it too ... on their own terms. We didn't have the right to just slaughter them. There was no question in my mind .... I knew down deep ... I had to follow my conscience and my K.H. on this issue.

One afternoon my father and I had gone out back to the field of tall grass behind the back yard with his loaded .38 revolver. At one time the field must have been plowed land because the ground was intermittently bulging with over-grown clods, making walking a tricky balancing act. Crows were circling and calling, unaware, high overhead.

My heart was opening its throttle as he took numerous pot shots at them. Squirming with nervousness, at first I didn't say anything. I fervently hoped he would miss them. But I knew I had to *do* something to get him to stop. I started talking to him, jabbering. I thought it might interfere with his concentration and aim. But he simply ignored my non-stop prattling. He kept on firing.

Now I was getting very anxious. My mind was sprinting to find an answer. I considered bumping into him, clipping the back of his knee, or jostling his hand. But that could create a stray bullet. A random shot could potentially strike another person, one of our dogs running amok, another animal crossing the property, or maybe even shoot my father in the leg. If I did such a reckless thing, he would strike me out of fear, anger, or frustration. Then my heart halted ... oh, no! ... He actually did wing a bird about forty feet above us. It tumbled swiftly into the tall grass which barely cushioned its fall. I cried out, "No!"

Before my K.H. could urge me to save the bird, I was already on my way. Rushing to it, holding back my tears, I stepped outside my non-assertive child self. I straightened my spine and forcefully demanded, "You can't let this crow die. I want you to take it back home. Treat it. I want you to save it. Then set it free!" He looked at me somewhat astonished. Then an almost bemused expression covered his face. I wondered, suddenly frightened, what that meant. But I stood my ground, my heart surging, expecting the worst.

I waited for his anger to explode, anger which always seemed to bubble under the surface. But to my amazement he didn't show it. Instead, he complied. I regarded him quizzically, not sure what to make of it. He gently scooped it up, adjusting its wings so they were folded at the bird's sides, located the bullet hole—a through and through—then took it back to the house. Upon inspection, he found the bullet had just barely nicked the wing bone and removed some feathers. He treated the wound with peroxide. Then he put the bird in a confined place where it could recover.

His chosen convalescent location surprised me. He put it in the four-by-six-foot, screened-in porch on the second floor, outside my parents' bedroom. I thought he would put it in the windowed conservatory/storage room on the first floor in back. But, then again, maybe the crow might have flung itself against the many windows in an effort to escape, furthering injuring itself. Its hospital site meant we all could enjoy listening to the ongoing beating of its wings against the door and screens and its incessant loud cawing.

Daily my father fed the bird corn and bird seed and gave it water … when he was home. My mother took over the task when he was on a sales trip. She dodged the claws, beak, and flapping wings of the thwarted crow. In this confined forest-green space the bird created a drizzled white and green Jackson Pollack canvas.

After the bird's month-long recovery, my father released it. It successfully stretched its wings wide, taxied down the front yard, and took flight with only a slight initial wobble. Then my mother and I dutifully carried a bucket of water, detergent, bristle brushes, and old rags upstairs into the screened-in porch to erase the excremental abstract decoration of its former patient.

My father never did punish me for my standing up for the wounded bird. I had no idea why he acted as he did but I was very glad he did. Sometimes he seemed to emotionally turn on a dime. Consequently, I never could be sure what he would do and what would happen as a result. I knew confronting him was, in general, a definite no-no.

In retrospect, I was astonished at myself. Saving the bird was very bold of me! I was so pleased and proud of myself for having had the guts to rise to the occasion. I had stood up to my father, openly expressed my wants, and risked punishment for doing it. I knew I'd have to nurture that exhilarating feeling because I had no conception of when that sort of thing might recur … if ever. Never relenting when principles were in question, my K.H. reminded me of what I'd heard Gandhi had said about an ounce of practice being worth more than tons of preaching.

The problem with having such an adrenaline-addicting moment was that it made me aware of a facet of myself and of a life that was possible. It was a stroke of promise that I thoroughly relished. I'd hold it near and dear no matter what ... and seek a reiteration.

CHAPTER 5

Impersonating His Desired Gender

I worked hard at pretending that acting like a boy really helped me secure my father's acceptance. But I knew way down in my gut that it didn't even penetrate the surface of his pre-determined evaluation of me. As I thought about it, it might actually have embarrassed him in front of other males. They might have wondered what was wrong with me for acting that way. It would have been something which would have reflected negatively on him. Having an inkling of this at the time, I had made a point of ratcheting my impersonation back several notches when around others. My father tended to be very concerned about being negatively evaluated. He had to be constantly "right" and "perfect" so no one could criticize him.

And, I was so torn because I wanted to be who I really was. I wasn't sure who that was just yet, but I *knew* I wasn't a boy. I didn't want to be one—although, boys did seem, at least in my observations of my brother, to get privileges which girls didn't get. Moreover, I knew my father was acutely aware that I was not a boy. Who was I kidding? And my presence as a girl, in spite of my characterization, was a constant reminder that I wasn't what he wanted.

But desperation pricked my thumbs as if I had fallen into a bramble of stinging nettles. I had to keep trying even if I had only a one-half of one per cent chance of succeeding. So I would use this ploy until I could find something better ... assuming there were something better. I had to entice him to somehow change his mind about me ... to find worth in me too *as I was*, not as I could have been ... *if only*.

My K.H. reminded me my father valued education, his making references to his own education having been stunted by his father. So

I decided to pursue the good-grade route. That was very easy for me because I loved learning. I was the proverbial little sponge taking in all around me, storing it, processing, analyzing it where possible, synthesizing it when necessary, and recalling it. Besides, getting A's rewarded me for being me. I didn't need his approval to know I'd done well. That felt incredibly good. At least I had one way to gain a sense of acceptance. Because it seemed like my only way at the time, I grabbed onto it with both hands.

When I finally let the boy masquerade drop ... with great relief, I strove to become as nearly "perfect" as a "mere" girl child could be. But that ran me headlong into two other obstacles. It was patently clear that he didn't want a girl AND I really hated doing the "sweet little girl" thing. With dwindling options, I fought with myself over what to do. Completely rejecting the female child stereotype, I took it on anyway.

There was no way I was the "little miss" in the magazine ads. I wasn't always clean and neat, playing only with dolls and doll houses, having tea parties, wearing frilly outfits, and demonstrating all white-glove military-etiquette with "Yes, sir; no, sir." And I didn't want to be. Instead, I was, despite my present emotional confinement, in the preliminary stage of becoming an iconoclastic little person.

Dolls were all right but my passions ran to learning to communicate with horses, observing insects and animals, teaching dogs tricks, collecting minerals I discovered, growing flowers, reading books of all kinds, doing puzzles, sketching, and wearing pants.

Once I found a praying mantis nest, which looked to me like a much smaller version of a paper-covered wasp nest. Putting it carefully on a box of dirt in the conservatory/storeroom to hatch, I checked it daily. I looked for any sign of openings in the nest wall. Then one morning to my delighted surprise, it was open. Hundreds of tiny, miniature praying mantises covered the box. What a miracle that seemed to me.

As much as I wanted to observe them, I couldn't leave them inside. They needed to start their new lives outside with access to praying mantis food, whatever that was. I took the box into the backyard and placed it near the terra cotta red, purple, and yellow chrysanthemums bordering our garden. It felt good to be making my own decisions, even small ones, and acting on them. While I hadn't really been part of their birthing process, I was at least a surrogate nanny, protecting them all until they could fend for themselves.

It was difficult being constantly at odds with what others expected of me. My father's expectations were diametrically opposed to who I was. Saying it was torturous not knowing which way to turn to make it better was an extreme understatement. I sometimes felt like I needed to wear wreaths of garlic to keep all my life fluids from being sucked out of me when I wasn't looking

At this time a young dark-haired "woman" named Rebekah joined my second-grade class. Wearing a thin, home-made dress of some non-descript color cotton, she was tall and slim, had breasts, a waist, and underarm hair. She was one of the saddest people I had ever encountered in my young life. She looked so uncomfortable and out of place seated at our small desks, with all her short, flat-chested, waist-less, relatively hairless classmates surrounding her. I couldn't imagine her joining us. I wondered if she was only now being allowed to attend classes. Perhaps she had come from a farming family that needed her to work instead of going to school. There were lots of farms around us.

When I looked at her, I would momentarily feel better about myself. But ... then, I would plunge into guilt for having made the comparison. She too must have felt unacceptable. She looked as forlorn as I felt. I regret not having made friends with her before she disappeared soon thereafter.

What was I going to do? That was the overarching question in my mind. What would my K.H. do if her father had laid that kind of "boy instead" baggage on her? In my more vengeful moments I pictured her with all her athleticism giving him a karate chop to the solar plexus to help him get his brain into reverse gear. Or I saw her pulling out her well-honed debating tactics I'd seen in so many movies. She could soften him up into retracting not only what he had said but also how he thought and felt about me.

Through her strength and conviction, perhaps, she could have convinced him that girls do have worth: that *I* have worth. I knew she would have done something to address the situation right there and then, where and when it needed to be done, in the driveway. Of course, I didn't ... and couldn't. I was in no position to question anything my father said or did. It was an implicit rule in my family that you did not question my father. I was very afraid of breaking that rule.

When I was a very young child, I was always looking to make my father laugh in order to make him like me ... even before I was informed I was "unacceptable." One time we were driving a short distance from our rental house in Madison, New Jersey, when we passed an African-American man walking along on the sidewalk. My father stopped the car and rolled down his window to chat with him. At home my father was always making prejudiced remarks and jokes against people of color, different nationalities, and various religions. I didn't fully understand them at that time. I just knew he thought they were funny.

The man came over to the window, leaned on the door, and they talked about work, the weather, and stories in the newspaper. When there was a pause in the conversation, I stood up and leaned my small body over toward the steering wheel to speak. My pudgy face creased with humor-inspired anticipation, I asked the man, "Do you work in a coal mine?" The man's faced blanched and my father sank into the driver's seat. It was obvious my father was not sure what to do next: ignore the situation, apologize profusely, or shove a sock into my mouth. I stood there in expectation, waiting for my father to laugh. He didn't.

When I was older and realized what I had done, I felt so contemptible that I had helped demonstrate my father's bigotry to someone who was undoubtedly experiencing it on a regular basis without need of my casual assistance. He may have even thought of my father as a "friend" before that incident. It wasn't my place to disabuse him of that notion. If I had been part of a twelve-step program, he would definitely have been on my list for making amends.

CHAPTER 6

Drowning in Betrayal

In our year in Leesport, we ate mostly inexpensive "comfort" food. My mother taught me to make pancakes, grilled cheese sandwiches, macaroni and cheese—when cheese still had a strong flavor even when melted, and made-from-scratch Swedish meatballs. Doing new things correctly gave me confidence that I could possibly do other things right as well. One Saturday morning for a lark I added a little green vegetable food dye to the pancakes to make them festive. My father would not eat green pancakes. I didn't get it. What difference did the color make as long as they were cooked properly? It was his way or nothing.

Food created other problems for me as well. This was a time when peas and I became mortal enemies. The odor of the peas reminded me of unwashed human bodies or the dogs' breath after they had licked themselves. Even holding my breath did not render them any more palatable. My highly-annoyed mother made me sit at the table until I ate them all ... however long it took. "I cooked them for you and you'll eat them. We're not going to waste food!"

Surprisingly, however, when my mother added the disgusting legume to her tuna casserole with Campbell's mushroom soup, diced celery, lemon juice, Worcestershire sauce, Tabasco, noodles, salt, pepper, and crushed potato chips on top, their flavor was disguised and they went down my gullet with ease.

I thought then it was too bad we didn't have the small, school cafeteria milk cartons at home because they were perfect receptacles for stowing rejected foods. The dogs, which would normally eat anything they could wrap their jaws around—edible or not—were of no help. Even they shunned my offer of this chlorophyll-filled "treat."

Exhibiting food dislikes in my father's presence was risky. I had to be careful especially with "creamed chipped beef on toast"—which my father often affectionately referred to as "SOS": "shit on a shingle" and *really* liked. No matter how long my mother soaked the chipped beef in water to remove the preservative salt, I found it unpalatable. Interestingly, the chipped beef, like many other products at that time, came in small glass jars with snap-on lids that could later be used for drinking glasses, like the ones for grape jelly. We had a lot of those. My K.H. urged me to swallow it because it wasn't worth the resulting difficulties. But to my taste buds it was like swallowing a tablespoon of salt. It made me want to puke.

My father didn't like anything that suggested "disobedience" to his strict rules which covered everything imaginable, including food. The food rule was you belonged to the "clean plate club." "Eat it!" he'd command me. "Eat it now, goddammit!" It didn't matter what it was or if I had been give too much to consume. His face would get red—his jaw muscles flexing—at my seemingly ignoring his orders. He threatened to get his leather belt and whip my legs with it. But I still couldn't swallow it.

When nothing seemed to work, he'd leave the table, stating, "You are going to stay here until you finish. Do you understand me? You are not to move from here until you have thoroughly finished your meal. If that takes all night, then you're going to sit there all night!"

As the evening dragged on, I was still sitting at the table in the kitchen struggling. He'd come back to check on my progress ... or lack thereof ... with belt in hand. At that point he'd finally appeal to my sense of guilt. Invariably he would start to rail about the "starving children in China." My K.H. halted me from following my first impulse to sarcastically suggest, "We can send this stuff to them so they won't starve." I did swallow the SOS but only after I had macerated it into an *almost*-tasteless purée and chug-a-lugged an eight-ounce glass of water with it. Even then, my gag reflex wanted to repel it.

Despite his strict rules about everything, my father did allow me to take advantage of our access to the country club pool as long as my mother was present. Because of our location on the club property we could use the pool when it was less busy. Around it was a five-foot-wide cement walkway that generally was hot to the touch. I had to hop on the balls of my bare feet, like a prancing horse, among the lawn chairs to get to a ladder to enter the pool. So often I just made a wide circle around it instead, slipping onto the cooler grass outside the walkway.

There was a five-foot high wooden, white and red lifeguard's chair stationed near the shallow end. One life preserver hung nearby on one of two hooks on the back side of the long building housing the four changing rooms. The pool ran from its two steps into the shallow end on the right to its eight-foot depth on the left under a diving board. After a month of having lots of swimmers, the water emitted the nose-stinging scent of chlorine. This was a pool I would never forget.

One morning before the club's guests arrived, my mother and I were at the pool where I was going to get my first swimming lesson. I never went into water higher than chest-deep. I didn't know what I'd be doing for the lesson and hoped it wouldn't require me to be in deeper water. I was so excited that I soon would be back-stroking, Australian crawling, and swimming under water all around the pool. Everyone else seemed to be able to do it. It was time I learned too. Johnny, the lifeguard at the country club, was going to give me my lesson.

Tanned, only slightly muscled, about six feet tall, with a hairless chest, squared jaw, light brown hair, and zinc oxide on his thin aquiline nose, he looked bored. His body language suggested he'd prefer to be eating a meatball sub with onions in one hand with a Pabst Blue Ribbon beer in the other while chatting with a lithe sixteen-year-old female rather than overseeing people in the water.

He was probably no more than eighteen but to my mind if he was a "lifeguard," he was an accomplished swimmer and instructor. And today he was going to teach *me* to swim! Actually, I didn't care who taught me to swim; I just wanted to swim ... now. He was handy; my mother didn't swim; and my father was working. In actuality, I would have been happy to have learned how to merely float, tread water, and dog-paddle. Since my father didn't expect me to do much, I pretended to be pretty casual about it all. But inside, I was full of anticipation!

Johnny was already in the pool when he had me enter the water. He was located where I knew I would have to strain to reach the pale aqua gunite bottom. I pictured myself as Esther Williams and tried to enter as gracefully as she did. Generally, I just slogged my way into the water. But today I was going to be Esther Williams "Junior" so I tried to act the part.

Having to meet Johnny at his depth precipitated cold butterflies flapping their wings against my stomach walls. As I arrived in front of him, I couldn't stand. I had to try to bob up and down, touching my big toe on the bottom to thrust myself upward again. It was too deep. I definitely didn't like it. But, then again, he was a swimming instructor and lifeguard, paid by the country club as such. He knew what he was doing. I should trust him.

He looked at me without any expression and got right to work. He placed a mop handle horizontally in front of me and motioned for me to grasp it with both hands spread out in line with my shoulders. Then wordlessly, he grasped the center of the pole and began moving around the pool at that depth. I flapped my legs in a simulated flutter kick. Occasionally he looked around to see if anyone else were coming over to swim.

I could feel the muscles in my upper arms and shoulders tighten as I tried to arch my back and still kick. I thought I'd seen that done. Okay, I started to relax a little. Maybe the depth doesn't matter. So this was how it is to swim. He's directing my path but I'm the one swimming. Wow! I'm actually swimming! This is a piece of cake. Johnny, look at how well I'm doing. You're a great instructor! And all in one lesson too!

If I had been Esther Williams in a movie, I probably would have fluttered my eyelashes at him. I looked at my mother not ten feet away in her bathing suit, soaking up the morning sun's rays. She was sitting in a webbed aluminum lawn chair reading her Rex Stout paperback mystery. I smiled. Oh, boy. I can do this. Look, Mom, I'm swimming! She looked up and smiled back. Looking disinterested, Johnny sighed and pulled me around and around in a small circle.

My mind was filled with Esther Williams looking so glamorous with every hair in place. Most people looked like drowned rats in the water. I did. Boy, I loved the movies. I couldn't wait to be a good swimmer like her. I looked at the wispy clouds in the sky. I was smiling to myself, daydreaming, as I rhythmically slapped my legs on the water.

Suddenly he let go of the pole. Straight down I went. Like a punctured bag of cement. I sank out of sight to the bottom of the pool. I swallowed a mouthful of water. Water rushed up my nose. As my bottom slapped the rough surface below, my heart cannonaded in my chest. I hadn't taken a breath! I didn't know I had to! My lungs started to burn. Where were my feet? My mind was racing. I had to get my feet under me. They seemed to be all tangled. I slapped the water to buoy me. Panicking, I was pushing sideward, not downward. I couldn't force myself upward. My feet were still under me ... some place!

The exertion made the pain in my chest worse. I screamed in my head, I can't breathe. I'm going to drown. Help me! Somebody, help me! I'm going to drown. No! No! No! Mommy! Please. See me! Mommy, save me! Daddy? Johnny? Somebody help me! Please save me! Where's Johnny?

I bent my head back and looked up. The pole was drooping in the water above and behind me where Johnny was. He pushed it away. My lungs were on fire now. My nasal tissue burned from the chlorine in the water. Mommy! Mommy! Partially facing the side of the pool, I focused my now inflamed eyes. Unlit flood lights were embedded in the wall in front of me. Was this the last thing I'd see?

Looking up again, I saw my mother's rippling image above. She was still reading, totally unaware of me. I felt as if I my body were collapsing onto itself. I had to breathe. I needed air. I saw Esther Williams dive under the water. She didn't come up again. My mind filled with flashing images of my father. He was smiling.

Hours seemed to pass. I saw an apparition. It looked like two protrusions. They were coming down into the water. In front of me they pulled me back. I was away from the side of the pool. Was I dying? Then something grabbed me under the arms. From behind ... haltingly, slowly, it brought me up to the surface.

Sputtering, coughing, wide-eyed with terror, I tried to breathe. But my breath didn't come. I let out a loud wail, expelling the little de-oxygenated air that had lingered in my lungs. But nothing was coming in to replace it! Did my lungs still work? I felt a little cold. Darkness was haloing my vision.

Suddenly gasping, I was grabbing short puffs of air. But I needed more ... I needed lots more. My lungs still burned. My head cleared a little. I was being suspended in the water. Johnny was holding me up. An odd expression covered his face. YOU! Semi-consciously I wrestled myself out of his arms. I shoved him away with repulsion. I had to escape from him. But I was still in deep water. I tried to scramble back to the shallow end. I struggled to get my legs coordinated. I had to get them under me. I had to get out of the pool.

But my knees buckled. I went down again under the water. But this time I touched the bottom with my big toe and pushed myself up, spitting out water. My legs pedaled toward the shallow. My cupped hands pulled water toward me. My feet finally managed to reach bottom. I was at chest-deep now. My legs unsteady, I fell forward again. Slowly I made progress. I began to walk-crawl on my hands and knees. I could barely keep my head above water. Slowly advancing on the little kid's-end, I found the steps where I collapsed.

Unrepeatable words I'd heard my father utter more than once came to mind. My mother came over to comfort me, not sure what had happened. I merely glared at him between heavy sobs. My eyes were daring him to come near me. I wanted to beat him about the head and shoulders with his mop handle until he was rendered unconscious. Then maybe he'd get to see what it was like to nearly drown.

I couldn't tell whether I was angrier with him than I was confused and panicked. What was going on? I didn't understand. Why did he let me go? Why didn't he say something—anything to warn me? He knew he hadn't taught me to float yet. He couldn't possibly have thought I'd automatically stay afloat when he let go. I had to float not to sink. What made him think I wouldn't sink and drown? Was this his version of tossing a kid into the creek to sink or swim?

Now wracked with tears, sucking in air in gulps, I sat on the second step, with my feet still in the water. I never said a word to him about it. But I fiercely longed to shout at him at the top of my lungs in my sodden rage, "You fugging, no-good lifeguard sunovabeech!"

My K.H. would have given him a hefty piece of her mind. And, maybe, she would have presented him with an even heftier swipe with her golf club to the back of his cranium ... just to get his attention. What he'd done was not only foolish but also exceedingly cruel. She'd make sure he knew it. After that experience, I wouldn't let *anyone*, even my mother, near me in the water unless my feet were firmly planted on the concrete beneath me.

My swallowing pool water was something I kept secret from my father. I knew he would somehow label my nearly downing as my fault: that I was stupid to think Johnny's pulling me around was really teaching me to swim; that no one can learn to swim in one lesson; and that I could have floated if I had wanted but I wasn't even trying. My mother, even though she hadn't witnessed it, likewise said nothing because my father would have chastised her for being stupid for not watching me every moment, not having been in the water with me, and just letting it happen. Because of that, my mother didn't report Johnny and his criminal incompetence to the country club management.

Later I imagined him being hoisted up by his "manhood" on the hook beside the life preserver. That would have served him right. He helped instill a fear of the water in me that day, something I had never experienced before. Years later I did learn to swim on my own, becoming an accomplished swimmer with life-saving training. The real K.H. was an adept swimmer, having been taught by her father ... a father very different from mine. Maybe it's a good thing my father didn't try to teach me to swim. Because ... maybe ... I really would have drowned under his tutelage.

From that day forward, now emblazoned across my brain in stenciled letters several inches high was a reminder of that earlier message to "be very careful whom you rely on."

CHAPTER 7

Outside Bullying

While I was at Leesport Elementary School, I repeatedly had unpleasant encounters with a slightly older, heavy-set girl named Ellen. She wore a large brace on her right leg. Apparently she had taken a dislike to me though I didn't know why. I had never spoken with her nor had any kind of interaction with her. The only time I saw her and her thin alter ego, Judy, was when the buses had gathered on the gravel play area immediately behind the three-story brick building to take us home.

When I was in line to board the bus, they'd wander over to me and start in, "Who do you think you are? You don't come from around here. You have *our* place in line. You have to move to the back of the line." Then they together would yank me out of line, push and pull me around for a few minutes, keeping up their tirade, before finally shoving me, laughing, to my bare knees onto the sharp rock shards at my feet. I didn't know why they didn't accept me. Could it be for the reason my father didn't accept me? No, he didn't want me because I was a girl. Could they feel the same? Or was I generally "unacceptable?"

What could I do? What should I do? I didn't know. How could I retaliate? Was I allowed to? Time and again for weeks I arrived home with bloodied knees, from which I still have the remnants of scars. Was I being punished for who I was? Or was I being punished because I didn't stand up for myself? As in every other situation, I never even said a word in my defense. I didn't like it one bit but felt stymied. My K.H. wouldn't have tolerated it.

My K.H. kept urging me to tell my mother about the ongoing bullying since these girls were taller and one out-weighed me. I was afraid to. Tired of witnessing my ongoing injuries and my reluctance to confront my abusers, my mother finally had had enough. She took the risk of telling my father. He was not happy to hear the news. I had created *another* problem for him. Somehow, after grumbling to himself and nearly dislodging the telephone directory pages, he located Ellen's father in the phone book. He called him, sounding barely tolerant. They made the arrangement that *we* would visit him this night.

Anticipating the worst, I was panicky and resistant about going. I begged to stay home. I didn't want my father to criticize or blame me in front of strangers, and, perhaps, in front of Ellen too. That would be too humiliating. He stated with irritation, "If *I'm* going over there because of *you*, you are definitely coming along with me and your mother!" My mother likewise didn't look eager to go but said nothing.

Once there, as the adults gathered in the living room to have their forced summit conference regarding my situation, I was required to go upstairs with Ellen. I followed her as she slowly thumped her way up the wooden stairs to her room. Her steel brace rang with each step as she grabbed the banister to keep her balance. Her ascent was awkward. In her room we avoided each other's gaze, saying nothing for a while. Then she tentatively brought out some of her few prized possessions which she then proudly showed me. With a half-inclined head toward them she indicated that we should share.

Surprisingly, after a short while, we settled into looking at her photo album. Page by page she did the commentary. She finished with, "This is my mom with me and my dog Sparky in the field behind our house. This is my mom holding me." A tear rolled down her reddening cheek as she croaked, "I miss my mom." As her face scrunched up, crying, I didn't know what she meant by that. All I knew was that her mom wasn't home while we were there. I felt tears well up too. She seemed to shrink into a figure so small, shy, and sad to me now. She no longer seemed so intimidating. I didn't know whether to put my arm around her or not. I was afraid she might take it as an embarrassing invasion of privacy.

This evening she wasn't displaying any of her typical physical aggression. In fact, we seemed to be getting along with equanimity. She was acting more reticently in her home than on the playground.

Coming away puzzled, I had a slightly more positive feeling about her. I hoped her kinder behavior here would generalize to the bus setting.

Maybe her sharing her crying would make things better ... or ... make things worse. I still had no idea how I'd defend myself against Ellen and Judy if things didn't change for the better. No one had allowed me to assert myself. Essentially I had "victim" written all over me in fluorescent paint.

What my parents learned was that Ellen had been born with a weakened leg and wore the heavy steel brace to try to support, strengthen, and correct it. She understandably chafed at having to wear it, feeling different, stigmatized, and the object of jokes and derision—"unacceptable." Her friend Judy was very thin because of some bone problem, maybe rickets. So the two of them were like peas in a pod, protecting one another.

But her aggression, was, perhaps, due more to her mother having died within the year. She and her mother had been close. She was not coping successfully with her absence. That left her father feeling helpless to deal with Ellen and her acting out. That was so sad. I couldn't imagine life without my mother. It frightened me to think about what would become of me if *my* mother suddenly left us. There would no longer be any reason for my father to keep me at home. Would an orphanage be my next residence? Or would I be palmed off on relatives? Would they want to take me if I were so "unacceptable"?

After that meeting, I no longer had a problem with Ellen and Judy which was a relief, especially for my knees. But my father's actions confused me. Had he actually stood up for me with Ellen's father? I mean, why would he have done that if I didn't matter to him? Or had I misconstrued the situation? Maybe he didn't really do it for me. My K.H. was inclined to think he had done it for himself—defending his family and himself as he was expected by society and his father and in keeping with his sense of control. But I could never tell for sure what to make of it.

CHAPTER 8

Getting Extravagant Gifts

Despite my father's strictness and seeming emotional distance, there were times when he would be generous to a fault, even truly extravagant. These out-of-character occasions tended to occur infrequently, mostly in my younger years, and only when my father was feeling particularly affluent and upbeat. But those occasions, irrespective of whatever prompted them, held a lot of meaning for me when they did occur. It didn't matter whether they were directed at my mother or me. I held them close to my heart. Perhaps he was changing his mind about us in general and about me in particular.

He bought my mother a Hammond electronic organ. She played it haltingly when not doing chores. It was in the small den off the living room to the left of the French doors. She even had lessons for a while to learn chording and coordination between the left and right hands and feet on the pedals.

My father bought my mother a yellow and green parakeet which she named "Mr. Peepers." In the evening when no one would be opening the French doors, Mr. Peepers would be allowed to fly around the room which he seemed to revel in doing. One time after circling the room three times, he landed on my mother's wine glass. Carefully perched, he tried to dip his beak into the pale gold liquid to take a drink. As he started to, he fell forward. My mother quickly knocked the glass over onto the coffee table top to keep him from drowning in her Chardonnay. She loved her little feathered friend. He would rub his short, curved bill against her cheek, returning the affection.

He always perched on her knitting needles as she knit-purled her way to creating a variety of stylish woolen garments: fancy-stitched pullovers, cardigans, sweater vests, scarves, mittens, hats, and blankets for all of us. Yarn was relatively inexpensive at that time so she worked continually on her projects. Surprisingly Mr. Peepers never defecated on her knitting. But he did, at least on one occasion, leave a white and black badge of honor on my father's shoulder upon landing there. It then rolled down the front of his shirt, forcing me to stifle a dangerous chuckle.

While my mother was very talented with knitting needles, she was likewise expert with crochet hooks. She even crocheted a white cotton bedspread in the complex popcorn-stitch pattern with a small, thin crochet hook and fine thread. Beautiful, it would have commanded a high price on the open market. I still have it, stored in a heavy plastic bag. Her knit goods always seemed to last for decades as long as we kept the moths sequestered elsewhere.

As an anniversary surprise, he had taken her to New York City to Carnegie Hall to see a performance by pianist-comedian Victor Borge, whom she loved from his 78-rpm albums. For this big evening my mother had gotten all dressed up in the only fancy dress she owned. It was an understated gray faille that had a scoop neck, long sleeves, fitted bodice with dropped fitted waist, and full skirt. With small pearl earrings and a drop-pendant necklace with a single fresh-water pearl, wearing black high heels and lacy black cotton gloves, she looked as if she had stepped out of the pages of "Vogue." She may not have had much money for a large wardrobe but she knew how to buy well and dress even better with what little she had.

He had bought her Princess, a seventeen-hands-high—approximately seventy inches at the withers—chestnut-colored, former-jumper with luxuriously long eyelashes and a penchant for chewing Tootsie Rolls. It was obvious that she and my mother had a special relationship. Since my mother was in the early stages of learning to ride with an English saddle, Princess seemed to be very understanding and worked with her.

She did whatever my mother wanted, while subtly indicating what did work and what didn't work for her. In response, my mother kept her previously-broken front right leg well-exercised. And she groomed her until she shone. Her perfectly toned muscles glinted in the sunlight, from her velvety nose to her luxurious long black tail.

Princess showed her gratitude by gently nuzzling my mother's face with her nose, causing my mother to throw her arms around Princess's lowered neck, close her eyes, and smile beatifically.

My father bought me a quarter horse I named Crackers. Because my father claimed she hadn't as yet been "broken," he bought a post-hole digger and built an eight-by-eight-foot enclosure constructed of split-rail fencing. In it he let her know who was boss about wearing a halter, bridle, and saddle and accepting riders. I was truly confused about this. When I first met her, she was saddled. I sat upon her as she was calmly led around with me on her back. I still have that picture of me on her, grinning from ear to ear.

My K.H. felt it was inappropriate for me to watch the ensuing fight between my father and Crackers because I would want to stand up for Crackers. That could be hazardous for me. My father told me, "Go away. I do not want you watching this. You can't ride her or even touch her until she's ready." What did that mean? I couldn't touch her in her stall or in the corral? That was stupid and cruel. How was she to know I loved her? I didn't care what he said. I'd do whatever I could to comfort her and let her know I was there for her as her friend.

As far as I could ascertain, he never hurt her physically with all the ropes he used to "break" her. But what did he know about "breaking" horses? Why did he have to pretend to know it all? It was going to be a battle of wills. I felt so bad Crackers was on the losing end ... no matter what. She too deserved to keep her spirit and self-respect intact. I later bemoaned the fact that my father had neither the knowledge nor the patience of a horse whisperer. If he had, it could have benefited not only Crackers but also my mother, brother, me ... and himself.

He had also bought two Great Dane puppies, which never looked like puppies to me with their huge feet. However, they certainly acted like them. They climbed all over everything, all legs and feet, scrambled up and down the stairs, and raced around the house from room to room, their long thin tails whipping everything off the tables they dashed past. They behaved as if they were being chased by comical devils. They had ravenous appetites, requiring numerous feedings of horsemeat a day. Fortunately mother handled that because I didn't want to touch the defrosting horse meat. It seemed sacrilegious and an affront to Princess, Crackers, and Red.

I suspect my father had gotten the dogs more for himself than for us though I didn't know why. He was always unilaterally deciding to buy animals. Irrespective, I loved them. The fawn one we named Stuffy, and the black one, Spooky. They had already had their ears cropped so their ears were wrapped with white adhesive tape to make them stand upright. That was a process I thought of as mutilation. I heard that some people did it themselves to their dogs without anesthesia. That was incredibly barbaric.

While cropped ears were for fashion, I felt that was no excuse. They were just pooches and our companions, not competitors at the Westminster Kennel Dog Show. I didn't approve of what was done for dog shows either. These big, sweet dogs didn't just act like puppies. They also acted like wood chippers. With great speed they gnawed off the arms of an antique mahogany chair with its petit-point seat one afternoon when no one was there to monitor their behavior.

My father wanted to let them run free. What? My mother and I directly stated our wishes to the contrary. What my father wanted, my father got. Our carefully-expressed suggestions, complaints, and disagreements held no weight in his decision making. My K.H. would have been even more forceful than I was in my argument: "It's too dangerous because of all the cars either going to and from the country club—or people traveling on the Pottsville Pike across the bridge next to the club heading toward Leesport proper—or those crossing the bridge toward Reading," the next town over, "and what if there are animal traps around in the preserve? What about people shooting game?"

It seemed to me like such a stupid, irresponsible thing to do. Walking them wouldn't have been that big a chore. If he didn't want to, I would ... or my mother would in when I was in school. Or, perhaps better still, we could have created a clothesline run for them out behind the house.

Unfortunately his pronouncement meant they could romp through the dark game preserve next door at will. This must have presented them with great expectations for smells and exploration. They ended up there any time they could. When you couldn't find the

Danes, you knew where to look. There were birds to uncover and foxes and raccoons and squirrels to chase ... maybe even deer. As dogs, they were oblivious of the dangers it presented ... but, incredibly, so was my father.

As we found out later, the person who managed the game preserve had placed some tasty treats among the dense undergrowth for non-game animals. These were things that pheasant or grouse, for example, wouldn't be interested in. Upon finding one of his hiding places, Stuffy and Spooky rooted it out and gulped down the treat. But, unbeknownst to any of us, it was meat that he had secreted there as bait for the foxes. It had been laced with strychnine.

While their torturous deaths were labeled "accidental," as far as I was concerned, my father was responsible—he murdered them as surely as if he had put his .38 to their heads. His behavior was unforgivable. Poor Stuffy, poor Spooky. Our dogs were found on their sides about twenty feet inside the preserve. Their eyes were wide open, with sardonic grimaces snarling their jaws. Their contorted front and rear limbs suggested they had died in grotesquely painful seizures. My big, beautiful, sweet babies!

How could my father not have known about it? How could he have not have checked before he let them loose? Traps? Poison? Being shot? Being bitten by a snake? Being attacked by a fox? Being bitten by a rabid raccoon? Being kicked by a deer? There were so many possibilities for the kinds of harm that could befall them. His impetuosity and lack of pre-planning led to other such instances. I wanted to condemn him to a fiery pool of magma for his floating lack of animal accountability.

CHAPTER 9

Learning the Past

As things ground to a halt financially once more, we had to sell some of our prized possessions, like a Victorian green velvet drop-side sofa, commissioned water-color Chinese portraits, as well as my mother's electronic organ. My father then borrowed money from a family friend, Tim Filson. We had known Tim for some time. He had left his Morgan horse, Red, with us and subsidized its feed and board. If my father felt embarrassed about owing him the hundred dollars, he never showed it directly. He did, however, avoid Tim whenever possible after that. I became the telephone operator who said he wasn't there. It was possible that my father also resented Tim because Tim liked and valued my mother as a friend. Perhaps that made my father decide that not paying Tim back was more acceptable. He didn't repay him.

This type of resentment had likewise happened years before in New Jersey when my father's friend Garry, who wore thick, black-framed lenses and had a built-up shoe because of a shortened left leg, visited often. Garry, who was blond, slight, and ran a hardware store, had found my mother a delightful conversationalist. He had shown her companionable attention whenever he visited which my father didn't like. My father tended to be very possessive and jealous.

My mother was five-foot-seven, slim with natural blonde hair with the slightest strawberry undertone that she wore in a shoulder-length pageboy. She had bright blue eyes, creamy skin, and a winning, ready smile. She used little makeup except for Tabu's Chili Bean lipstick, a red with a slight brownish tinge that set off her coloring. She wore it slightly over her upper lip line to cover a tiny scar that embarrassed her. It gave a slight Hollywood look which added further to her appeal.

Ironically the only "valuable" thing we saved from being sold was the television. This was good for me because I was just hearing about Senator Joseph McCarthy. He was the Republican Senator from Wisconsin who rocketed to public attention in the early 1950s. He alleged that hundreds of Communists had infiltrated federal agencies, including the State Department. His accusations heightened the nation's anxiety about the possible spread of world Communism.

But instead of seeing him as a demagogic, anti-Communist crusader, I saw him only as he "appeared" to be at that time daily on the screen: an honest person trying to expose corruption ... today's "whistleblower." He appeared to be unfairly persecuted at the Army-McCarthy Hearings by head counsel for the Army Joseph Welch (who said, "Let us not assassinate this lad further, senator. Have you no sense of decency?").

Later when I discovered who McCarthy really was and what he had perpetrated, it was mind-blowing. I'd never forget that example of how appearances can be deceiving especially when I didn't know the history and context. I later recognized that it further suggested that I should not accept things at face value. Skepticism, research, and critical analysis would be useful friends in assessing what was perception and what was reality. My K.H. was continuing to make me aware of this important point.

Because of the saved TV, it was by this time I had seen K.H.'s films, "State of the Union," "Adams' Rib," and "African Queen." In each of her characters she exercised her freedom of speech and encouraged thinking and reasoning about any topic of concern. "African Queen" was my favorite because she was an unmarried missionary in the Congo who constantly fought against passivity and accepting whatever came along. Relentlessly, she did whatever was necessary to achieve her goal of sinking the German naval ship, the *Lüisa*, during World War II.

This approach was unlike my father's. My father accepted whatever came along ... by way of his father. He had indicated he had never wanted to be a salesperson. His goal since childhood had been to go to college, specifically Cornell University, to become a veterinarian. He talked about it all the time. He was constantly rescuing animals. He brought home all sorts of menageries for my mother to care for. But it was he who tried to suture a baby rabbit which had been torn open when attacked by a neighborhood dog, with sewing needle and thread. Despite all his careful ministrations, the bunny died of shock. I put it in a shoebox and buried it with regret for its early, traumatic demise.

But there was no way he could ever become a veterinarian, something which I think he had finally and sadly recognized. Life as he knew it appeared to be outside his control and stacked against him. He seemed to have no idea how to break free even if he had thought that it might be a possibility. Down deep I think he knew what the score was. He had to play the game shackled hand and foot.

His father dictated that his three boys would work for the Parker Pen Company—period—because he was a sales executive at their Manhattan office. His sons always obeyed him to the letter ... or else. I never knew what the "or else" represented, and maybe they didn't either. Unvoiced, veiled threats, I found later, can be lots worse than voiced, explicit ones. As a result, they always snapped to when he issued his commands.

He was like General George S. Patton, "Old Blood and Guts," directing troops in the punitive expedition into Mexico using the first motorized military attack. He strapped the bodies of the enemy dead onto the hoods of the three Dodge Brothers Model 30 touring cars. I could picture my grandfather doing just that, in riding boots with a riding crop, arrogantly slapping the outside of his right leather boot.

Instead of Cornell, my father was allowed one year only at the private Hofstra College of Liberal Arts on Long Island. Before his being moved into Parker Pen, he worked at a Curtiss Wright aircraft manufacturing plant in New Jersey. This was during World War II. He had been disqualified from serving in the military because of a "headache problem." He had sustained a severe head injury when a freight elevator door slammed on his skull, nearly killing him. It was at Curtiss Wright where he met my mother.

In her senior year in high school she had to leave to help support her family. Not having her high school diploma embarrassed her greatly. Always fascinated by rocks, minerals, and volcanoes, she had wanted to go to college to become a geologist. But that was out of the question financially at that time. In later years, I took the GED for her. However, I don't think her now having a high-school equivalency had any effect on her feelings of overwhelming inadequacy. But she did continue to read about aspects of geology all the time ... and dream.

Even worse for my father, as I heard later, he had also had been given an appointment to West Point by a senator friend of the family. His father promptly nixed it. This guaranteed to further keep his son close at hand and under his large thumb. Reveling in having control, my grandfather enjoyed showing his power over others, especially his sons and their families. He did this physically as well as psychologically.

CHAPTER 10

Stability Spiraling Downward

When I was four years old, my parents wanted to build a three-bedroom wood-frame home of their own in Summit, New Jersey, several blocks from the hospital where I had been born. It was to be in this new, attractive development which was rapidly being built out. It boasted large yards and comfortable distances between houses.

This was nothing like the Levittown planned community in Pennsylvania which was made up of 17, 311 little boxes nearly all the same and all crowded together. Our development was, instead, like an early suburb promoting spaciousness but close to everything. It made no pretense at being a "community." Houses were individual but within current architectural expectations.

There was no need for Levittown's strict rules to make sure residents kept their properties attractive and well-cared for. Everyone did because they wanted to and for the area to stay desirable. My father's building enthusiasm was infectious so we all looked forward to the day we would move in.

To put the plan into motion my father secured a building loan ... from his father. The white house with the brick front façade went up quickly. Amazingly, I even got the octagonal window in my closet at the front of the house that I'd asked for at the blueprint stage. That was so much cooler than a square, rectangular, or round window. I could watch my father mowing the lawn. I could enjoy the tulips, forsythia, crocus, and daffodils in bloom in the spring. I could even check out what was occurring on the sidewalk ... to see if any kids my age were playing there. Then I wouldn't miss a thing ... through my special, personal, private window. I was so pleased with it.

Everyone was thrilled with the result. My mother planted a large, blooming lilac on the left side of the paved driveway. Then she constructed an extensive—twenty-foot long and four-foot high on a sixty-degree slope—rock garden of pansies, begonias, spring bulbs, violets, phlox, daisies, and snapdragons in the back behind the house. It started from behind the garage, ten feet from and below the kitchen window. This allowed her to look out on it and admire the colorful result. It was fifteen feet from my swing set from which I continually tried to touch the sky with my Buster Browns.

Even after several torrential rains washed out her green-thumb handiwork, she rebuilt it stone by stone, adding new plants, making it even better than before. She had a real knack with plants which she loved.

So proud of her floral accomplishment, she showed it to everyone. Soon she was becoming friends with other women in the neighborhood. This made her happy because she had craved female companionship. She was just twenty-seven. In too many of the places we had lived, there were few, if any, young women around with whom she could associate. In Leesport, I tried to make up for that by having coffee with her in the morning before my school bus arrived. I didn't like coffee. I tried to act mature as we sat across from each other at the kitchen table. It couldn't fly. While I'm sure she appreciated my efforts, she couldn't really talk with me as she would with another adult female. What could I seriously share with her? "See Spot run. Run, Spot, run" from the *Dick and Jane* series of school readers?

Unfortunately my father began frequently to intrude, uninvited, on her coffee klatches before he went to work. It didn't matter whether they were at our house or at her friends' houses. He'd walk in, get some coffee, and sit down, asking. "What are you talking about?" Maybe he longed for that kind of casual, friendly coffee conversation too.

He didn't have any friends then so far as I knew. Furthermore, he never seemed to do anything with other males, except his brothers on rare occasions. But his frequently joining my mother sucked some of the life out of the kitchen interactions. Surprisingly, he never seemed to sense the perceived presumptuousness of his presence.

My mother told me she resented their not being able to have a private talk about whatever she and her friends wanted—including their respective husbands, families, or things they wanted to do but had yet to achieve. Moreover, his being there at others' houses tended to make her feel guilty about not being back at her own house every moment.

Later I wondered if his appearance might have been a passive-aggressive indication that he thought she should cease what she was doing and return to her homemaking. While meeting for a cup of coffee became less enjoyable for my mother and her friends, at least my mother was finally able to have some adult female-female conversations. She poured out her discontent to me. At this age I became her confidante.

In the house she enthusiastically did all the interiors. She wallpapered the living room that ran the length of the right-hand side of the house with a pale green figured paper with a subtle Japanese feel. She added potted bamboo, a ficus, and jade plants in brass pots to bring the outdoors in. Open-weave beige drapes completed the look.

She painted the dining room on the left side of the house a Chinese lacquer red. She liked Asian decoration and had a tall Chinese porcelain lamp, a handmade black wire bird on a branch inside an open frame, a large porcelain incense Buddha, and two watercolor portraits, one of a Chinese emperor and one of his empress. Drapes in a muted, antique gold and the red, blue, and gold-colored ersatz-Caucasus rug complimented the walls. It all came together with life, making the meals there feel more companionable.

My father soon bought a loud, squawking, biting-everyone-but-him parrot he named "Polly." To my mother's chagrin, he insisted on keeping it in the kitchen to be away from drafts. But, he didn't consider the effects of the gas used by the stove. Despite my mother's care, even giving it orange juice by the teaspoon for the Vitamin C when it developed a respiratory problem, the bird died of pneumonia a short time later. I'm not sure anyone in our household really knew how to care for a tropical bird. Why not? This seemed so unforgivable to me.

For the moment all seemed calm in our *own* little house. We had a sense of permanence, security, and belonging ... finally. My brother Wally was happy in his crib and I was happy with my closet window. Then, suddenly the roof caved in.

My grandfather decided "on a whim," he said, he wanted to buy another black Cadillac. He moaned, "It's so awkward taking the money out of the savings account and investments because they are getting such good interest and I don't have that much cash handy." That was a wink, wink, nudge, nudge to his son.

Consequently, he did what seemed perfectly reasonable in his Machiavellian logic. He called in his loan to his son. It didn't matter that the only way my father could conceivably repay the loan *immediately*, which my grandfather demanded, was to sell the house. This was not something lost on my grandfather. As they say, "the Lord giveth and the Lord taketh away." And he definitely was allowed to be the Lord overseeing this family.

My K.H. would have balked, renegotiated, or just plain refused. After all, what was his father going to do? Sue him? He couldn't get blood money from this proverbial stone. To my mother's unbridled amazement and rage, it apparently had never occurred to my father to do anything but lie down, roll over, and comply as he was commanded to do. With sadness and frustration my parents put the house on the market, continually showed it, finally sold it, and found another rental. We were like gypsies, constantly on the move with our caravan wagon. Of course, with each move, we had fewer and fewer belongings we would need to move.

Slowly all the furnishings that were meaningful to my mother had drifted away. My mother said good-bye to the first friends she had had in a long time. This even included Sarah, Keith's mother from next door on our right. Keith was a four-year-old, pint-sized bully, trying to take away my toys when I was playing with them on my driveway. I was willing to share as long as he'd give them back when I was ready to go in. He wasn't.

Of course, I couldn't touch his possessions. He screamed his head off whenever he didn't get his way. I wanted him to disappear and leave me alone. My mother and Sarah had some disagreements about Keith while we were there. But she liked Sarah despite her bratty child. My mother and I were convinced Keith would grow up to be a bratty adult.

So as soon as we moved and my grandfather got his money, he bought his new car to add to his growing fleet. In retrospect I thought that I really had to give it to him. He knew how to keep his sons off-balance. He had them by the short hairs. He had them where he wanted them. They were better trained than circus seals.

The new owners of our house cut down the lilac which infuriated my mother. She had driven by to check on her beloved first real home. She never forgave them for it. She had nurtured and loved the bush. She gave it motivation to bloom profusely. This way she could stroll outside to sniff its divine fragrance and snip a few twigs to always have a vase full of its lavender blossoms in the house in season.

My mother displaced her fury from where it really belonged ... with my father and my grandfather. My grandfather had in one swift action essentially castrated my father and removed our first true sense of safety and belonging. My father was left unable to keep a roof over his family's head ... or be the master of his own destiny. He was again pointedly reminded who was the real captain of his soul.

CHAPTER 11

Confronting Polio

Shortly after our move, a polio epidemic struck northern New Jersey. This was years before a polio vaccine was invented by Dr. Jonas Salk that saved millions of lives. It was a terrible, indiscriminate scourge. My Uncle Dennis and Aunt Rachel's three children and my brother and I were among the many hundreds in our area infected.

Four of us had non-paralytic polio. We had stiff necks, backs, and limbs; muscle spasms; raging headaches; sore throats; and high fevers which lasted about ten days. But Denny, their oldest, contracted paralytic polio (specifically, bulbar polio) that affected his brainstem. This left him no longer able to breathe on his own. He had to be in an iron lung, a negative pressure ventilator, which would "breathe" for him externally.

I couldn't imagine how awful that would be. I pretended my lungs didn't work and held my breath. Without that control all I could feel was panic. Just listening to what sounded like a large bellows whooshing in and out, breathing for him, was frightening to me. What must it have been like for him ... and his parents?

I don't even know if he was conscious because I couldn't tell looking up at him from standing below the long, bulky metal cylinder on wheeled legs. What if the electricity went out? How would they power that respirator? What could his parents or anyone else do to help him? It was too terrible to consider. I couldn't wrap my young mind around it.

I didn't know how my aunt and uncle could stand seeing their beloved five-year-old Denny like that. He was like a small ragdoll. I wondered how they could feed him and bathe him since he couldn't breathe on his own outside the iron lung. The iron lung did have air-tight portholes in its sides for doing some of these things, but I didn't know how they worked. How could his parents touch him, kiss him, and hug him to show him he was loved?

What agony they must have gone through knowing that if he lived, he'd be stuck in this steel-drum-like monstrosity with only his head and neck protruding, with a mirror above later on so his parents could see his face. This would be for the rest of his life. He would be with hundreds of other children in a similar situation in this special polio ward at their hospital. This is when I first thought about becoming a doctor to help these children.

Recently I read that one person was in an iron lung for sixty years before she died at age seventy-two. There were no options available to my aunt and uncle. It was whatever it was. Given that, perhaps it was both terribly cruel and a blessing that he and they didn't have to stand it for years and years until he was seventy-two. Leaving their spirits nearly at the breaking point, he died a short time later.

As a result of the infection, their middle child, Darren, had developed a leg disability which took years of physical therapy to remedy. Their youngest, Deidra, had developed epilepsy which interfered with her activities for the rest of her life. My fever floated around 105 degrees for a day or two resulting in a cortical functional abnormality. According to my EEG, there appeared "paroxysms bi-laterally in the temporal regions" of my cerebrum.

In English, there were intermittent large spikes of electrical activity on both sides of my brain ... *almost, but not quite,* suggesting epilepsy. What that gave me instead was fierce migraine headaches that increased in intensity as I grew older. It took decades to get them under some control.

I have no idea why some of us contracted the non-paralytic type of polio and some the paralytic type. My brother, who escaped unscathed, and I were so much luckier than so many others. My heart went out to my aunt, uncle, and cousins. Later on I wondered how my father could possibly have coped emotionally and financially with the necessity of ongoing medical care for his children *if* we had sustained severe disorders as a consequence. Before he slid over his own emotional precipice, he might have been able to handle it. In fact, such a crisis might possibly have forced him to act in his own family's best interest, rather than in his father's.

CHAPTER 12

Controlling Through Pain and Fear

One family story recounts how when my grandfather arrived home from work one day at their Basking Ridge, New Jersey, farm complex, he found my grandmother, a short, plump, kindly woman, kneeling into a lower kitchen cabinet cleaning it out. Instead of announcing himself, he walked up behind her, raised his highly-polished brown Florsheim wingtip shoe, and kicked her into the cabinet with a chuckle. Apparently this was not the first time he had been physically abusive to her. Though at the time few of the family would say they knew about it for sure.

To his utter amazement, as she scrambled out of the hole, she got her hands on a large kitchen knife which was lying on the counter above her. She flung it at him with all her strength. The blade landed tip-first into the wall beside his head ... mere inches from his face ... vibrating with a distinctively lethal hum.

Later, as I learned more family secrets, I suspected *one* of the reasons he abused her, besides his being a natural-born tormentor with a cruel streak a football-field-wide, was that he "had to" marry her after getting her pregnant with his first son. He was one who never let go of a grudge. In fact, he was likely to hold it against her forever ... until death they did part. If anything really mattered to him, it was maintaining his supreme control over *everything and everybody* in his life.

My grandfather's sister, Ella Mae Framstead, was nothing like her brother and the only one not under his control so far as I could tell. The grandchildren called her "Grandma Ella" and our parents called her "Frammie." Heavy-set, diabetic, Christian Scientist, and very loving to children, she frequently invited me to her small apartment for tea and some heavy dessert. Her favorite was lemon meringue which she made such that it was almost too sweet to eat. It made me wonder if she only passed a whole lemon over the top of the pie, proclaiming it "lemon meringue."

Her living quarters were old-fashioned with faded flowered wallpaper, lacy white antimacassars on the backs and arms of all the overstuffed chairs upholstered in faded, flowered-print fabrics. On a walnut three-shelved bookcase she kept a black, hollow metal figure of an elephant she called "Suki." I played with Suki all the time. Because I loved it so much, the last time I saw her she gave it to me. And I still have it.

Frammie, however, had one habit that was very risky. Being very frugal, she saved even tiny leftover portions of food in the refrigerator. I didn't know if that was just a habit or she had little money. Shortly after my last visit, she ate some long-refrigerated peas which led to her undoing. She had lost track of when she had stored them and developed food poisoning from them. Since her religion used only prayer for addressing illness, totally eschewing medicine, she died a slow, painful death. That was a great loss. She seemed to be her own person—and a sweet, accepting person as well.

My father's mother, Geraldine, was like Frammie in many ways. She was a sweet, sharing person whom I loved to be around. My father was the spitting image of her in his younger, slimmer days as demonstrated in early photos of him fishing for sailfish with his brothers off Long Island. She had always shown her love for and acceptance of me. She praised me with how pretty I looked in a new dress—"That is such a pretty color on you"—how well I had done on a coloring project—"Those trees look like real trees"—how well I read *Winnie the Pooh* to her—"Oh, I can picture Pooh and Piglet together when you read"—or how well I helped her with the dishes—"Those dishes really look clean and shiny."

My grandfather, on the other hand, asked why I was doing a stupid twirling dance step when I showed him my new attire, pointed out I had colored outside a line in one corner of a picture, corrected my mispronunciation of a word as I read, and told me, with disgust, I had missed a particle of food on a dish I had washed.

It was a given that no matter what I did, I would never reach the bar he set. As I approached the top of the achievement ladder, he would release a new section of it and raise it higher. I was inadequate until he conferred the title of "adequate" upon me. It later seemed that it was something like his knighting me for my level of acceptance to him. I never felt the sword blade tap either of my shoulders to confer the title of "acceptable" on me so I knew where I stood. I was beginning to see where my "unacceptability" came from.

When my grandfather wasn't around, she was assertive in her own quiet way. Once when I visited, she offered me a slice of jelly roll but warned me, "Don't tell your grandfather about this. He won't like anyone else eating his cake." Even at my tender age, I could tell that if he thought she had given any of *his* precious jelly roll away, especially to a child, she would have paid for it. I didn't want to consider how that would play out. It was our secret. I smiled and crossed-my-heart-and-hoped-to-die. I promised I would never tell him *anything*—not even if he tortured me—and I meant it. Unknowingly at that time, I would later have the chance to prove it.

Another time when all the male grandchildren were going swimming in my grandfather's bulldozer-created pond, I was left without anything suitable to wear. They had simply stripped off their outer clothing and had gone swimming in their tighty-whities. As a girl, I couldn't exactly do that irrespective of having nothing to show. "Wait," Geraldine said, "I have an idea so you can join them." My grandmother went to her bedroom where she collected two of her large silk scarves. One she wrapped around my chest and tied in back and the other she looped through the center in front and tied around my neck.

"There," she said with a large grin, "what do you think?" I smiled too. It was not exactly a Coco Chanel creation but with my shorts it would work like a dream. As a result, I got to have fun splashing around in the muddy water, walking on the slimy bottom with everyone else. There were some things I didn't want to miss. I have no idea if those silk scarves were cleanable after that. Her typical thoughtfulness allowed me to have that mud-coated experience.

For years before my father's mother had died, Geraldine had wanted to have her ashes scattered around the several willow trees she had planted that arched over this artificial pool of mud in Basking Ridge. She had carefully nurtured those trees as they grew in strength, height, and swaying elegance. She would even sit under them in their dappled sunlight, talking to them. They helped her keep her sanity. It was a shame that they couldn't have helped lower her high blood pressure as well. But to counteract the stressful effect of my grandfather, they would have had to have been grown from magic seeds.

When she died, my grandfather disregarded her wishes. Her ashes were not scattered near them. They were not scattered anyplace at all. Instead, in a downright refusal to accede to her wishes, he had her embalmed. Her body was then entombed in a mausoleum, someplace nearby. My Aunt Rachel told me that no one really knew exactly where so they couldn't easily visit her. It was always *his* way or no way. Even at the end, he had sucked the last molecule of life out of her.

As I later learned, with most physical domestic abuse you rarely see it occur. I never actually saw anything against my grandmother that I could label "abuse." However, there was one time, after my grandmother died, when my grandfather summoned his three boys and their families to make a command appearance at his new, beautiful 200-acre farm on a mountain top in Saxon's River, Vermont, that seemed to fit the definition of "domestic abuse" to a T.

Once everyone was present, he told his sons to line up all his grandchildren on the large brick back patio to shake hands with him. Most of the children who were younger than I looked perplexed at this. They seemed to wonder if maybe they were going to get a special prize from their granddad, maybe get a ride on the hay wagon or a visit to the horses nearby. Down the road a quarter of a mile lived a pinto horse named "Riley" which I had already met on my own and lusted after. The grandchildren were in for a surprise, not a prize. This was not my first time so I knew what was coming.

"Daddy, pleeeeeeeze," I pleaded, looking for my father to finally rescue me from the approaching torment. But my father stood with his brothers on the sideline, eyes cast downward, once again impotent, trying to blend in with the trees and shrubs bordering the patio. "Just shake hands with your grandfather," he urged. He looked embarrassed as if his having to talk me into it was a reminder of my unacceptability. Moreover, I was humiliating him in front of the family patriarch who expected so much more from him.

Years later I came to understand my grandfather's perception at that moment: Wasn't his son supposed to be the ruler of his house and family? Didn't he make sure everyone toed the line? What kind of wimp parent was he if he couldn't get his young child, and a female to boot, to do what he wanted, especially in front of his father and his brothers?

The three boys looked helpless, like mule deer gathered in the middle of a rural dirt road caught in the headlights of a logging eighteen-wheeler. One thing was obvious. If they wouldn't do anything to stop what was about to occur, their wives, our mothers, certainly didn't dare to either. They were in the delicate position of having to pick their battles carefully with my grandfather. Maybe they would intervene if he were going to boil their children with cabbage and potatoes for an Irish dinner. But anything less was questionable. Unassertiveness was the rule and strictly adhered to ... or else.

He expressed his thoughts about women: "They're only good for one thing. Their place is in the kitchen and the bedroom. They have nothing useful to say. It is the men who have the brains and make the decisions so women shouldn't worry their pretty little heads about anything other than housekeeping, meals, and children." If he didn't listen to his boys, he surely wouldn't listen to their wives.

I didn't want to cry, to show my fear. But I didn't want to shake hands with my grandfather either. I was hanging on by my fingertips. What should I do? If I cried, he got what he wanted. If I played stoic, he would do his best to make me cry. "Heads I win, tails you lose." No matter how I responded he got what he wanted.

From his plastic, webbed lawn chair, he called us one at a time to approach. I was first. The routine was each of us would march up to him and wait for him to put out his huge ham hock of a hand. His hand would so totally engulfed our tiny hands that they disappeared within his grasp. Then, staring us in the eyes, as if to deliciously register the first sign of discomfort, he would start to squeeze ... and squeeze ... and squeeze.

When he extended his hand to me, I looked to my father again. Begging with my eyes, I asked for a special dispensation. My six-foot, one-hundred-ninety-five-pound father looked like a cowed little boy, standing in the corner embarrassed for having just wet himself. Resigned, I turned back to my grandfather and lightly placed my hand in his. And held my breath.

As the vice began to tighten, I vowed I'd hang on. I'd outlast him. I wouldn't give in to him. But that impulse lasted only a minute as the pain became unbearable. I automatically went into panic mode. I struggled to get free, my hand pulling, and pleading, "No! Please. Don't. Let go! No! Please! Please!" My K.H. shouted at me, "Don't struggle! Whatever you do, don't struggle. You'll only make it worse." Tears welled. But even as I tried to blink them back, they ran down my red, contorted face.

My grandfather just smiled. His intensely glacial blue eyes were unemotionally still locked on mine. "What's the matter?" he asked, his voice dripping with insincere sympathy. He was daring me to say something. I swore I wouldn't. I'd told my grandmother I wouldn't even if he tortured me. I stayed silent so he squeezed even harder and harder and harder. The bones crunched together and the tendons stretched to their limit. Finally, as he released my throbbing, purple hand, he smiled at me again. I wanted to thrust a wooden stake into his atrophied heart.

My K.H. would not have tolerated this for one moment. She would have taken a running leap at my grandfather, knocking the air out of him with her tennis racket, sending him head flying over butt off his throne onto the bricks. Then standing triumphantly over his flattened fat body, she would have placed an athletic shoe on his chest. Swishing her russet hair out of her face, she would have asked no one in particular, "Any questions?"

Unfortunately his being beaten by anyone—but especially by a thin, angular, no-nonsense woman—would have only escalated his need to make sure he would regain his power and stature. It was imperative that everyone know that *no one* would *ever* challenge him. The image pleased me all the same.

CHAPTER 13

Marrying His "Evil Twin"

The way my grandfather ruled his fiefdom he brooked no obstruction by disagreement or action. My parents had to kowtow and do his bidding. Since he obviously didn't like children, I could more easily avoid him most of the time. Children were useful to him in that they did give him further leverage in dealing with his sons and their wives. He had a tool bag full of all kinds of tactics to keep his sons quailing.

For one Christmas he had given my mother a Ruger pistol that looked something like today's P944. It was stainless steel with a four-and-three-sixteenth-inch barrel. At the time my mother was using target practice as a way to gain self-confidence and control. She really knew how to ease off the trigger and was getting closer and closer to the bulls'-eye at every practice session. She was very pleased to receive it, thanking him profusely for his generosity and thoughtfulness.

Then one year later, to her shock and dismay, he told her, "I want the Ruger back. I want to do some shooting." Demanding she give it back, he showed that it didn't matter to him that he had given it to her as a gift. He had decided he wanted it for himself ... period.

Of course, his being wealthy meant he could have bought as many of them as he wished without making even a dent in his financial status. But that was not how it worked with him. What he wanted he got. Since it wasn't worth the repercussions from him and from my father to argue or refuse, my mother returned it to him with a peculiar kind of resignation when all the families gathered in Vermont. There were no role models here for being your own person except for my grandfather. And he was his own person in spades.

To say I didn't like him was an understatement. But I didn't fear him in general, at least not the way my father and two uncles did. I wondered why they acted as they did around him. Did they obey him to curry favor with him or to get some acknowledgement of caring from him? Maybe it was to get a hint of some twisted manifestation of pride in them? Maybe to get a respite from his demands, their humiliation, impotence, and pain? Maybe all that and more, but they also seemed scared witless of him.

Before moving to Vermont, my grandfather had taken his second wife. Divorced, Mimi came into my grandfather's life as his housekeeper. As soon as Geraldine had died of a stroke in Basking Ridge, Mimi had slipped between his sheets. Remarkably, she looked a lot like John Fitzgerald Kennedy with his heavy-lidded eyes, his general facial characteristics. She also had a certain formidable quality. Her brunette hair which had gray strands was worn back, pinned in a bun at her neck. With a heavy-set body, she still had a semblance of a waist and the bosom of Jayne Mansfield. She proudly displayed this prodigious physical attribute with her flesh straining against the tight fabric of her halter-tops.

Like my grandfather, she knew precisely what she wanted. She knew how to get it. And she went after it with gusto, no holds barred. This meant you had be on the alert at all times and steer clear of her whenever you could. She definitely had her own version of a K.H. in her psychological corner on which she acted. But her K.H., as I later considered it, was more a Hannibal Lector.

Shortly after she married my grandfather while still in New Jersey, Mimi took me to New York City at Christmastime. This was specifically *without* my mother—which struck me as odd. Her goal, she said, was to buy me a doll. She had her sights set on a large, very expensive doll with long golden, curled hair, at the unique, high-end FAO Schwartz. It was legendary. It was, in fact, the most famous toy store in the world, crammed with innovative educational and fun toys.

As we entered the store, I saw life-size stuffed wild animals created by the German teddy-bear maker, Steiff. There were lions, tigers, and a giraffe. Mimi, I wanted to shout, forget the doll! I want

63

one of those lions instead! Of course, I wouldn't have dared to have uttered such a thing even in jest.

I had difficulty picking out a doll because I didn't feel right about asking for something—especially something so pricey. Besides, in all honesty, I didn't want another doll. I had one or two that I'd had for a while. Dolls were no big deal. Consequently, she chose one for me. It was wearing a finely tailored light blue, high-quality cotton dress. It had lace around the white Peter Pan collar and white buttons down the front. The skirt was box-pleated. It was even nicer than some of my own clothing at that time. It also had white socks, black leather shoes, and a change of wardrobe. The eye-lashed eyes opened and closed depending upon the position of the doll. I didn't feel right accepting this gift. But I knew I couldn't say "no" to Mimi.

Before we left, she offered to let me talk to Santa Claus. That seemed like a good idea. I had a mental list of things to request for my family. My father had not yet broken the jolting news to me that the fat, hairy elf in red did not really exist, much less give me presents. Slowly I walked over through the red-and-white candy cane roped lane. I walked right up to him then hesitated a moment, inspecting him. Something was amiss. Rather than let me continue my surveillance, he reached down and picked me up. As he put me on his capacious lap, I howled in sheer panic.

This wasn't Santa! This was just some big fat guy in a crimson velvet suit. He had Santa's large black, gold-buckled leather belt; white rabbit furred cuffs; a velvet hat with rabbit trim and pompom set at a jaunty angle; and was wearing shiny black patent leather boots. He had a beautifully waved white beard and hair to match. But this wasn't Santa who was putting his hands on me! I didn't know who this guy was but marveled at the gall he had. He was sitting on Santa's special chair, pretending to be him. I howled louder. He rolled his eyes and quickly shoved a pair of pink, rounded-tip plastic scissors into my hand and unceremoniously sent me on my way ... out of his ear shot.

Mimi didn't say anything about it. I had to give her credit for that. I sniffed to myself, too bad it wasn't the *real* Santa. But I never said anything out loud. I had never forgotten my lessons about being careful expressing myself. But this trip seemed so strange to me. I never understood why I was being given the royal treatment by her. I was old enough to wonder if she was going to do that with each of her new "grandchildren." Why me? She didn't know me. She surely didn't love me. Maybe that was her way of trying to make rapid inroads into the inner sanctum of his family.

I found out later that she had taken my Aunt Rachel and her three-year-old daughter, Deidra, to a fancy restaurant. She ordered a pricey meal for the toddler. And when Deidra didn't eat her expensive meal, Mimi went ballistic. Shouting in the restaurant at my aunt, she said, "I spent good money on that meal and she didn't even eat it! That's the last time I spend money on her." My understanding was that was also her last attempt at bringing the wives and grandchildren into her fold. I wondered why she hadn't tried to bring my mother in too.

This incident reminded me of when my father's mother took me my first real restaurant in the Morristown Hotel in Morristown, New Jersey, some fifteen miles from Basking Ridge. From a menu full of choices, Geraldine suggested Manhattan-style clam chowder and a sandwich. I didn't yet know what clams were. I had no idea to what degree I would have welcomed them in any other form. But in the tomato-y soup, they were delicious. Being in a restaurant where I was treated like an adult made me feel very mature and sophisticated. I have since wondered how it would have worked out if Mimi had been the one to take me instead.

As it turned out, Mimi and my grandfather were perfectly matched on their levels of kindness and sensitivity. When in another of our homeless episodes, my father asked my grandfather if we could spend an undisclosed period of time at his Vermont farm. Once again my father was trying to get us together financially. But, I wondered, what about our pets at the time? Were they going to make the trek with us? My father decided he didn't want to bring our Afghan hound, Hassan, and cat, Peoples, along. Instead he boarded them in New Jersey at a veterinarian's kennel.

Our pets would have been no more thrilled than we were about arising at 2 a.m., being packed into the car, and riding for hours and hours without a pit stop. That was my father's routine. He would drive and drive until we arrived. It didn't matter how many of us screamed for a bathroom. He'd yell to us, "Hold it! Hold it!" We stopped only when we needed gas.

I suspected my grandfather likely objected to our bringing the animals along. This was even though we had to stay in the small apartment above the large, red, wide-board, six-stall carriage shed and sleep on cots. Were he and Mimi saying something by not inviting us into their house with its excess of bedrooms? My father had arranged to have our mail forwarded to Saxon's River so he expected there would be no problems with receiving those specific vet bills. He had taken on a sales job at a nearby Bellows Falls' electronic organ showroom. This provided him with a paycheck with which to handle them.

He received regular updates on our pets as well as boarding invoices. But for some reason he was in arrears in paying the vet. That fact made me wonder if my grandfather was "helping" us out by charging his son rent for our quarters and meals. Blood may be thicker than water but for him everything had a price. My father's paycheck never seemed to go very far. As expected, the vet was demanding a payment. The next thing my father knew he didn't hear from the vet. A second week went by and he still had no letter from the vet. We all were getting very concerned.

Upon investigation, my father discovered that Mimi had held back the last two vet bills from us. My father called Massachusetts. The news he received was heartbreaking. As a result of our continuing non-payment, the vet had euthanized our pets. The shock, grief, and overwhelming sense of betrayal made me want to retaliate physically. But what could I do? I was still too young and too small to do anything meaningful.

When my father learned of the death of our beloved furry ones, he questioned Mimi. She had already slipped into the role as his step-mother. "Oh," she said, her polite smile in place, "[Golly, gee] I must have somehow forgotten to give them to you. Sorry. Were they *very* important?" She did everything but flutter her eyelashes in mock sincerity at him. Standing beside my father, I felt the full force of what she had done. I wished her dead.

Swallowing his disbelief like a tablespoon of uncooked oatmeal, he made a point of not registering a complaint with his father.

Challenging or accusing Mimi would only bring a plague upon him and us. Instead, my father packed us up to leave shortly to go to New Jersey. We had no pre-determined destination in mind. What did it say about my father that he couldn't even protect his own dog and cat? He looked deflated. He was further defeated. Once again my father confronted the fact that he had little control over his life.

Before we left, my mother and I went into my grandfather's large strawberry patch. It was loaded with ripe berries singing their come-hither song to us. We had been told in no uncertain terms that the strawberries were "off-limits" to anyone but my grandfather. That order was too inviting not to disobey. So in bidding him and Mimi a fond farewell, we stuffed our faces with the scrumptious fruit, giggling. We looked like chipmunks, with red juice running down our chins.

"Huhr," I mumbled, "hab anothuh," and pushed a plump fruit into my mother's partially open mouth. "An ooh too," she mumbled back at me, chuckling deep in her throat because nothing could pass what crowded her mouth. Playfully she shoved another into my now-packed oral cavity. It was our pathetic attempt at momentary revenge. In actuality it was rather cowardly and we knew it.

Later I thought it would have been so much more meaningful if we had marched into the house and told him point blank what we were about to do. Then when we did it, we could have really relished it with our heads held high. Of course, raiding his strawberry patch didn't do anything to assuage our devastating sense of loss. By stabbing us in the back, Mimi cleverly got her obvious wish to have us leave as soon as possible.

Sometimes, when I thought about my grandfather, I wondered if what went around would come around. I was about to see that sometimes it does. As one not prone to visit doctors for anything short of a tiger having ripped off his leg, my grandfather certainly did not consult a physician for a cough he developed in his sixties. Having been a heavy smoker of unfiltered cigarettes since childhood, he expected some coughing now and then. But now he was coughing all the time, looking as if he couldn't get enough air. His fat face turned apoplectically purple. His pale eyes bulged. His voice was getting hoarse. This finally prompted him to see a physician for a diagnosis. The diagnosis was lung cancer.

However, by the time he did seek to discover the cause of his problem, what had been a single tumor had multiplied and spread throughout his left lung. He promptly had surgery to remove the lung. Then, when he felt back in control, he left the hospital to resume his exploitation of his sons and their families. But eight months later when he was having some movement difficulties with his legs, he checked back with his physician. This time he discovered that his lung cancer had metastasized to his brain.

Even knowing I was being uncharitable, I was not saddened when I heard about it. It was difficult to grieve for someone who oozed the threat of pain and torment from every pore, seemingly enjoying its effect on others. When he went back into the hospital, he lay white against the white pillowcase and sheets. He was thinner, gaunter, and less imposing. Tubes went into his arms and nose and came out of his other orifices, some emptying waste into a large glass container beside his bed.

And when he finally died, I felt nothing except the hope that he had met his end writhing in some screamingly, horrifically, excruciating way. In reality, I had no idea how the end finally came to him. I suspected he was probably made pain free to cruise in La-La land through the use of intravenous opiates until his respiration stopped. I wondered, somewhat sarcastically, if someone had put a crucifix on his forehead if it would have burned his flesh.

Still the image seemed so fitting not only to the way he had lived his life but also to the psychological holocaust he had created and to which he had subjected his sons and their families. Years later as a more empathetic person, I still can't say I regret my feelings about his demise. He was probably the product of his own dysfunctional family too. Still, it would have been kinder if he had cooperated with Death and shuffled off this mortal coil a lot sooner than later. It could have saved a lot of grief for a lot of people who did not deserve it. I wondered if his sons and their families would now re-gain their independence. Considering their many years of aversive conditioning by him, I suspected they would remain stuck in neutral. It made no outwardly apparent difference for my father.

While my grandfather was in the hospital for his second stay, my Uncle Dennis took one of his children with him and drove eight hours straight to visit his father for the weekend. Then he drove back eight hours straight to go to work the next day. He did that every weekend until my grandfather died. While praising him, Mimi cursed the other two sons for their not doing the same. It was as if they could possibly duplicate the feat, either time- or money-wise. My father certainly couldn't have done it.

Once when Dennis sent a very personal card to his father, Mimi upbraided Rachel for not having signed it too, "Your name should have been on it. You insulted Dennis's father, showing you didn't care."

Rachel tried to respond, "It was an intimate father-son sentiment. My signature did not belong there on the card."

To this Mimi responded, "It wasn't all *that* intimate. You were just being cruel and thoughtless, showing your disregard for him." Mimi was as good as my grandfather at turning things around to suit her. She was practiced at squelching any independence or assertiveness in those over whom she had control. My Aunt Rachel was sure Mimi was communicating all her negative perceptions to my grandfather, poisoning his mind against certain members of his family as it served her purposes.

CHAPTER 14

Staking Her Claim Through Their Hearts

Interestingly, as I later discovered, if any of his sons had hoped for even a small token of the father-son bond or something from his huge estate, they would have a long wait. As he lay *non compos mentis* in the hospital, he was barely conscious. Despite his cancer-ridden brain and his body having been pumped full of morphine, he was still conscious enough to be very susceptible to any suggestions "lovingly" made to him by his new wife. Reports by his sons indicated he could refuse her nothing. He wanted to believe anything she said. She had astutely made sure of that.

Shortly before my grandfather died Mimi had taken it upon herself to have a new will drawn up for him. This new one totally contradicted his old will which had existed for some thirty years. The old will had left everything to his sons in the event his first wife predeceased him. This new will, however, totally eliminated his sons and their families as beneficiaries. There were *no* exceptions. Even Uncle Dennis's weekly efforts to comfort his father before he died had no impact on the will's language. His sons would get zilch from him. Instead, it left every piece of personal property, real estate, bonds, bank accounts, investments, and pension to Mimi ... and to her alone.

Did he truly comprehend what he was doing? Did he truly intend, in his impaired capacity, to disavow his children and their right to an inheritance for their lifetimes of doing his bidding and showing their caring? He signed the document. That later struck me as so strange.

I long wondered how legal his signature could have been given his medically questionable mental state upon signing. But no one seemed to question it at the time. At least, no one brought suit against it. But the harsh reality was that Mimi now had the money to fight any and all suits his sons might bring against her. She could outlast them for decades to come so why would they even try. They didn't. Apparently, their legal retreat was the better part of their financial valor.

As a result, nary a monogrammed towel, an ashtray, or photograph was to be had by anyone but Mimi in remembrance of my grandfather. No one received any of the many gifts his sons, their wives, and his grandchildren had given my grandfather over the years. This included my mother's Ruger which was given her even before Mimi's arrival.

However, what my mother and I heard years later did give us some comforting smiles. It was a touch of revenge. After my grandfather died, Mimi went through the motions of getting him into the ground. She then sold the lovely Vermont farm and its hundreds of acres of profitable waving grain. With "her" inheritance she moved to Florida. But she was not alone.

Before she moved she had been on the train back from Manhattan, where she had been to my grandfather's office at the Parker Pen headquarters. Heading to Bellow Falls, she had met the married owner of a string of Cadillac agencies in Vermont. There and then they had arranged an assignation. This was the start of a lengthy affair. They then finally moved to Florida to set up housekeeping together.

Every six months he traveled on vacation to Vermont to visit his wife. Despite Mimi's coaxing and cajoling to get him to get a divorce, he made no move towards doing it. He tried to placate by telling her it would be "soon." But how long could Mimi, of all people, accept the feeble and insincere indecisiveness of "soon."

After years of trying to make it legal, she went for the sympathy vote. She ran her own Cadillac into a tree in a nearby park. Demolishing the front end of the car, she put a large dent in the tree. She also fractured her collar bone. To be at her side in the hospital, he raced back from Vermont. But as soon as she was released to go back home with a nurse in tow, he flew back to Vermont. He had to finish his vacation with his wife. Apparently his wife wasn't sufficiently bothered by their living arrangement, still benefiting from it.

Months went by before Mimi decided to call him, threatening suicide. Always with a purpose and a plan, she timed it down to the minute. Timing was everything. She was good at it. She expected him to arrive on his white stallion of a Cadillac Eldorado just before she actually carried out the deed. Giving herself some leeway, she finally turned on the gas and stuck head in the oven. But this time she miscalculated. Her plan went awry. He didn't show up in time. She would not be whisked away in her lover's arms on his mighty steed. All that remained of my grandfather's money, some of which she had lavished on her lover, went to her children by her first marriage.

Her only son, Ben, and his wife, Lisa, were into key clubs and other group-sex gatherings. I remember when her daughter-in-law was in Vermont dressing for her flight back to Washington, D.C. She was wearing Bermuda shorts and a knit shirt but no underwear. I wondered at the time if she were readying herself for any potential action on the plane, like the "Mile High Club" I'd heard about.

I figured Mimi's will provided her two daughters, Molly and Nadine, with a higher standard of living. It probably provided her son with access to more orgies. I don't know for how long. Sometime afterward, Lisa divorced Ben and married Molly's husband. She had been having an affair with him for many months. She later opened a pastry shop. I can't help thinking that my grandfather moldering in his grave would have snickered at this ironic turn of events.

CHAPTER 15

Encountering More Valleys Than Peaks

In Peapack-Gladstone, New Jersey, we snagged one-half of Maple Cottage to rent. Maple Cottage was well-known. It was on the one-thousand-acre Kate Macy Ladd Estate, also known as "Natirar" ("Raritan" backwards, named for the Raritan River that meandered across the property). A very large residence on Peapack Road, it was originally designed by Mrs. Ladd as a convalescent facility for women. Convalescence was later moved to the huge main residence after Mrs. Ladd's death. Maple Cottage was then split in half and leased out.

Our half had a three-sided screened porch where I roller-skated with my keyed, shoe sole-clamped roller skates. This is also where my mother hung her wash which turned into stiffly flapping sheets of fiberboard in the winter. Inside the front door was an eighteen-by-eighteen-foot rotunda with a hardwood floor and a large wooden fireplace on the right-hand wall—the wall which now divided the house. At Christmas time my mother decorated the mantelpiece with a snow scene I'll always fondly remember.

Using navy blue crêpe paper as the sky with silver glue-on stars, she built hills of newspaper covered by cotton batting. Everywhere my mother placed yarn-clothed pipe-cleaner people skiing, sledding, tobogganing, and singing in groups. Real evergreen twigs stood in as trees. Using a mirror as a frozen pond, she had her people skating as well. I always marveled at how she accomplished both realism and fantasy which let me project myself into the scene and enjoy the fun and community.

In truth, I could forego Christmas trees decorated with strings of popcorn and cranberries, colorful lights, holly, mistletoe, evergreen wreaths, and presents. It was her annual winter scenes that always made Christmas for me. Years later she expanded her scene to include a Santa's workshop, eschewing pipe cleaners to create full-bodied two-inch elves which she dressed in felt costumes. She built miniature furniture, tools, and toys. She decorated the interior of the workshop with tiny paintings and flower pots. She also had a barn for the reindeer, complete with fence and hay. Santa sat on his chair at his desk reading his list of naughty and nice girls and boys. When, towards the end of her life, she could no longer create this seasonal presentation, I truly missed it.

Beyond the fireplace was the downstairs lavatory with black-and-white floor and wall tile, white pedestal sink and toilet. The living room, dining room, and kitchen were on the left in that order. The windows of the living room and dining room looked out onto the porch. The kitchen which opened on to the other end of the screened-in porch was a narrow, galley-style but efficient. Counters, sink, and stove were all along the outer wall. Storage was above and below the counters. The refrigerator was just inside the door from the rotunda to the right. And the clothes washer was on the left wall, backing to the dining room.

In the center at the rear of the rotunda was a grand staircase with expansive white steps and wide walnut balustrades. They started in a tight spiral that curved sensuously outward and upward. Separating at the second floor, they formed a railing around the opening to the first floor. The three bedrooms were on the right moving toward the front, starting with Wally's room, mine, and then my parent's.

The long banister from the second floor to the first was very seductive. It seemed to sing its siren song of a heart-pounding, fun ride. The only problem was that my inner thighs could not sufficiently grip the wide but thin railing well enough. Trying it once, I nearly slipped off, hanging over the hall to the kitchen. Awkwardly struggling to regain my upright position, I decided that was enough. I couldn't be sure I wouldn't fall completely off the side if I raced down again. I didn't want to tempt fate.

While we lived there, my brother developed pertussis, whooping like a crane and barely avoiding death. Again it was only through my mother's twenty-four/seven care that he survived. Our two dogs which were running free killed the cat that belonged to the Murchisons who lived in the other half of the house. And, I attended two different *private* schools.

One was Miss Gill's School on Bernardsville Mountain, part of Gladstone, now called Gill St. Bernard's. The other was Far Hills Country Day School in nearby Far Hills. Both were non-sectarian, co-educational, exclusive, and expensive. They boasted a "rich school experience for individual pupils" academically and physically with small classes and direct teacher-student relationships. One of the buildings where I had classes at Miss Gill's looked to me like an old army barracks with bead board all around painted white. At Gill School we often had to sing the school's signature song, "If I had the wings of a turtle dove, back to old Gill School I'd fly. And there I would play with the students. And there I would stay 'til I die.'"

When I was at the Far Hills Country Day School, I played an angel in a small pageant they gave. I also acted like a devil as I flexed my K.H. attitude. One day in a room in the main part of the house we sat on the floor and watched a puppet show. White, wraith-like marionettes appeared inside a miniature fireplace. They danced around for a while to music then vanished up the "chimney" at the end. After the twenty-minute performance, we were herded out of the room. Ringing in our ears was a warning, "Do not look in the fireplace."

Always curious, I decided to risk it. When everyone else had left, I stooped down and looked up into the opening which would have been the flue. But I couldn't see anything. Of course, I was caught *in flagrante*, reprimanded, and given some trivial punishment. But I didn't care. I had thought it more important to investigate. I wanted to see for myself, to possibly discover something special. I felt bold disobeying what seemed to me to be an arbitrary command. Neither school nurtured independence at my young age so my rebelling felt good. My K.H. inner voice was making her presence known ... and I liked it.

Later I discovered that these schools were the launching pads for important people, movers and shakers. They claimed as alumni/alumnae numerous members of Congress, governors, ambassadors, and business tycoons. Unfortunately I was at each for

75

only a few months. This meant I could never benefit later from networking opportunities with former-classmates who now populated the well-to-do, adult in-crowd. But my father could say, omitting the particulars, he had allowed me to attend two exclusive schools.

Also while we lived at Maple Cottage, I was flexing my risk-taking by trying new things and seeking new adventures. I climbed a tall, large-trunked maple tree to see how far I could ascend. When satisfied I had conquered the tree, I started my descent. Using branch after branch as a handhold or foot placement, I made my way down. I was making great progress until I grabbed a rotted branch. It snapped off in my hand. I hurtled twenty feet to the hard-packed ground below, breaking my wrist. The tree was in the yard across the gravel driveway from what used to be the estate's two-story library. Tad and Nancy Dovell lived there with their two daughters, Terri and her younger sister, Frances.

While my mother and Nancy became good friends, Terri and I became inseparable. We even hiked across the back fields over a mile to the Kate Macy Ladd residence. There we climbed the rolling, precisely-mowed, grassy hill to look in its tall windows and gawk at its expensive interiors. After circling what seemed like a brick battleship to locate its entrance, we found an attendant to ask if we could look around inside. Entering through the white columned marble foyer, we were escorted into the empty main living area on our right. This was where residents could come to read, play games, and converse. My K.H. was urging me to explore.

There we saw a very high ceiling, rows of tall windows, ornate plaster moldings, large, gold-framed oil paintings, and tables and lamps. Scattered around the hardwood floor were old-fashioned wooden wheelchairs with woven-cane seats. If it hadn't still been a convalescent home, where we would have disturbed patients if we looked elsewhere, we would have eagerly explored more. I wanted to peek around every corner to see what I could discover.

One time when Nancy was showing my mother their house in its entirety, she included the spacious attic over the dining room and kitchen. It had only a temporary floor of wooden planks placed somewhat arbitrarily above the rafters and Fiberglas insulation. After having viewed the nooks and crannies of the attic, my mother started walking back to the attic door. But then the plank on which she stepped shifted its position.

She fell. Landing in a sitting position on the plank, she had one foot under her. Her other foot had plunged straight through the insulation and plaster ceiling of the dining room below. Hanging beside their ornate brass-and-glass chandelier was my mother's still-shod, long leg up to her hip. Tad raced to the attic to help Nancy and my mother disengage herself. Fortunately only my mother's ego was bruised. Terri and I had just entered the house as it happened. We were shocked into gales of laughter to see the unplanned addition to the room on our left.

I was thinking about my mother's fall as I hit the ground beneath the tree. I landed face down with a huge splat. The radius of my left wrist protruded at an acute angle. I hurt all over. I could barely breathe. I felt faint. Tad and Nancy weren't home so I had to go for help. I had to keep shaking the shock-like feeling away. In a daze, I held my left arm in my right hand and wandered back across the Dovell's yard and then the gravel drive. Once in my house I began to search for my mother. Moaning repeatedly, I managed to call in a strangled monotone, "I think I broke my arm. I think I broke my arm."

Initially, when she heard me, my mother didn't believe me. She told me she had actually pooh-poohed what I had said. Consequently she took her time coming to find me. Standing alone in the rotunda, I was alarmed. I called and called. My wrist was throbbing as I waited for her to answer me. For some reason I had expected her to race out immediately from wherever she was ... to find me ... to see what had happened ... to rescue me. But she didn't. Fear gripped me. Was she there? Who would help me?

Later I asked myself why she pooh-poohed what she heard from me. Why didn't she believe me? Why didn't she come to check on me right away? I had never played this game. I had never cried wolf. I didn't understand. I was in considerable pain. I felt sick ... and I felt betrayed.

She finally sauntered out of the kitchen, hands still wet from doing dishes. She had a small smile and looked as though she were ready to disabuse me of my notion. When she came closer, she saw the damage and stopped smiling. It was obvious that I wasn't exaggerating or mistaken or playing games, or whatever thing she had thought. She quickly packed me into the only vehicle we had available to us at the time. It was her 1931 Model-A Ford which had been "given" to us by my grandfather. That became my ambulance to the hospital.

This was a classy little black four-door sedan with black leather interior, a burl dashboard, and a "trafficator." This was a metal arm which would swing up from a hanging position below the driver's side mirror. It projected and flashed to indicate the appropriate turn and stop hand signals. Amazingly the car could reach sixty-five mph if you could find a road without traffic or a traffic cop.

But as great as it was to look at, it was equally terrible to ride in, *if* you didn't want to jiggle anything that shouldn't be jiggled. Its very firm suspension and narrow tires jarred my severely-deformed wrist fracture. I had to fight to stay conscious. I was constantly on the verge of throwing up all over the black carpeted flooring. Trying to ignore the pain, I cradled my arm in a bath towel on my lap.

Once at the hospital, no one talked to me. No one asked how I felt. Was I nauseous or scared? Was I on any medication? Was I allergic to anything? Had I had ether before? No one explained what I should expect: this is what we're going to do and how we're going to do it. My father wasn't around to find out and tell me anything either, assuming he would have done so. He was on another of his sales trips. I thought he should have been there for me at that dire moment. My mother comforted me. But she had no useful information about the procedure—at least, nothing that satisfied my need to understand what lay ahead of me.

Next I was escorted into a room. There they stripped me naked to the waist. My chubby upper body was exposed for all to see. They lifted me onto a table to lie flat on my back. Surrounding me were doctors and nurses clad in white masks, coats, and caps. They were all hovering. They ordered me to comply with their commands and actions. "What are you going to do?" I asked, frowning with a quivering lower lip.

"We're going to fix your arm," someone replied matter-of-factly from someplace out of my sight." "I know, but *what* are you going to do?" No one bothered to reply. I wanted—needed—to know more. "What are you going to do?" I said it louder. No one responded. Tell me more! I shouted silently as the figures in white scurried around me. My K.H. would not have stopped there. She would have kept demanding information until she was satisfied with what she heard. I wanted to know more but didn't know how to get their attention or what else to ask.

Without a word of warning, they lifted a large black rubber contraption from behind my head. It started moving toward my face. They were gathering around like vultures. I immediately forgot all about my excruciating pain. Fear took over. It gave me adrenaline-surging physical strength. I never knew I possessed such a thing. I turned into a young Hulk from the comic books ... without the green hue. I screamed as loudly as I could, "No! No! No!" I twisted this way and that. Arms flying, I tried to maneuver my way to get up, to get off the table, and out of there.

They didn't expect this "inappropriate" display from a patient. I obviously had no sense of medical decorum. They wrestled with me. They tried to hold me down without grabbing my broken arm. I was like some poor calf being roped and hog-tied. I was about to be taken to the slaughter. Where was my father? Angry faces and voices enveloped me. "Stop moving!" they shouted fiercely, impatiently. That only solidified my resolve to get away from them.

"Let me up. Let me go. Get that thing away from me! Get away! GET AWAY!" I shouted as loudly as I could. I was using my good arm over my head to bat the object away. Chaos ensued.

Another nurse, hearing the melee, rushed in to help them restrain me. In my mind this had become a life and death struggle. Daddy! Daddy! Please help me! Mommy! Please! They finally overpowered me. They shoved the black object roughly over my nose and mouth. The mask firmly in place, there was a hiss suggesting gas. A sickeningly sweet smell filled my lungs, and world.

Dissolve to black ... fade in to gray. I was abruptly conveyed into a void with no dimensions. In the foreground was a large white diamond outline vibrating rapidly. A skeleton slowly moved toward it, as if to go through it. It moved on an invisible wire from overhead, like clothes on a dry cleaner's automated moving rack. It was moving, moving, moving toward me. I waited for it to reach me. But it never did. In the background I could hear a soft chant of what sounded like "gittle-a-go, gittle-a-go, gittle-a-go" over and over again. The skeleton kept approaching the diamond. I screamed and screamed and screamed. I'm going to die. I know it. Then all went black.

When I came to, I found I had vomited all over myself. That was frightening. What if I had vomited with that mask on? They never asked if I had been nauseated before they had pinned me down. Did ether make you sick to your stomach? Was I sick from the shock and pain? Or was it all of the above or something else?

Later at home, I felt outside myself. I was looking down at me. I was conscious, moving, and talking but I was also on some astral plane, observing. My arm hurt but in an ethereal way—not as before. The white plaster cast was heavy. It ran from my knuckles at the base of my fingers, encircling my thumb, to just short of my elbow.

My mouth tasted sour from vomit. Things worsened when I found I couldn't brush my teeth. The combination of ether I was still exhaling and my toothpaste made me vomit all over again. How would I rid myself of that disgusting teeth-covered regurgitation from earlier at the hospital? I had little choice at this point. I decided I would try brushing and gargling with baking soda and water until I had rid myself of this revolting after-effect. It was days before I could go back to real toothpaste and feel that my mouth was truly clean.

I vowed to myself, mentally shaking my fist to the heavens, that when I became a physician, I would never—*never*—be that cruel to anyone ... and especially not to a frightened child. In retrospect years later, I wondered what had happened to their Hippocratic Oath of "First do no harm"? Where was their empathy? They were acting like automobile mechanics changing a fuel pump. They treated me like the engine area under the hood. As a physician, I would tell my patients everything they needed to know to fully understand. I would comfort them to ease their anxiety. I'd never treat them so pragmatically and heartlessly. They were not to be like objects to be "medically" manipulated and ignored.

CHAPTER 16

Embracing a Brief Encounter

After three months of that sweaty, smelly plaster surrounding my arm, I was finally to be through with it. The doctor sawed it off. Phew! That was so disgusting! I couldn't wait to scrub my arm until it no longer reeked. It smelled of something having crawled inside and died there. To celebrate my release my mother suggested we go for a picnic. A picnic! I was more than ready for this fun idea. Of course, I'd have to be careful for a while with how I used my now-unprotected left arm.

We drove toward Bedminster in her Model-A, with our basket of lunch goodies on the front black bench seat between us and a blanket in back. Just after turning off Peapack Road, she revved up the motor and headed up a steep grassy hill on the left side. Like being on a roller coaster approaching the summit, our backs were pinned to the seat. We climbed quite a distance before she angled the car to the left, parallel to the road, and set the handbrake. We spread the blanket beside it.

She had prepared a child's culinary feast: tuna sandwiches, hard boiled eggs, carrot and celery sticks, real lemonade, and homemade chocolate-chip cookies for dessert. The sun was bright, warm, and made me feel at one with the universe. There was the scent of hay from the field over the hill. It fragrantly permeated the slight breeze which kept us comfortable. Bees buzzed all around the daisies, red clover, purple aster, cone flowers, phlox, and buttercups. They surrounded us in abundance. I tested to see if my mother liked butter by putting a buttercup blossom under her chin. It shone yellow; she did. It was the kind of day that made me certain all could be right with the world from there on out.

We soaked up the sun and watched yellow and pale blue butterflies check out the flowers. After about an hour, the sky began darkening. It was whipping itself up into a frenzy of precipitation. Towering, dense, dark-bottomed cumulonimbus clouds seemed to appear fully formed from nowhere. They further blocked the sun. Hastily packing the car, we turned it around, and eased back down the hill, very glad the brakes held.

By the time we were on the road, the sky had unzipped itself. It loosed heavy droplets and high rotational winds on us. Thunder erupted. Lightning struck some object up ahead. It was an eardrum-rupturing crack. Immediately we saw what had happened. A large tree on the left side of the road had been hit. The high-voltage strike had split, splintered, and collapsed the tree across the road. We were left stranded behind a thirty-six-inch diameter trunk. There was no way we could either move it or drive around it.

We sat there in the battering rain for a moment, contemplating our options. My K.H. indicated we should look around for a house or driveway. Already having noticed a gravel driveway a few yards back, I suggested we go down it. If we found a house, we could use their phone to call the county for tree-hauling road assistance. Backing up and turning right, we drove down what seemed like a long, shady, tree-arched promenade.

At the end was a white mansion with a circular gravel drive. It was elegantly secluded by maple trees, dogwoods in bloom, and a twenty-foot-long lattice draped with sweet-smelling lavender wisteria. Against the foundation was a variety of attractive flowering shrubs. There were aromatic azaleas, rhododendrons, camellias, peonies, hybrid tea roses, Japanese painted ferns, hostas, and bearded and Siberian iris. Even under the tree cover, the plants were being pummeled by the heavy rain. Trimmed boxwood in the shape of globes sat in heavy Grecian urns which stood on either side of the front steps.

Hopping out of the car, we sprinted to the door. It was a large, solid wood, six-paneled door. It was painted dark green. In the center was a huge Victorian brass knocker. As soon as we rapped, a liveried butler answered. He bade us enter despite our sogginess. He then disappeared to alert the "master of the house." Just running from the car to the front steps, we had gotten soaked. Our clothes were dripping on the foyer's highly polished hardwood floor.

Suddenly a middle-aged man, about five-foot-ten, with medium brown hair, and a pleasant smile appeared. He was wearing a dark green velvet smoking jacket, paisley ascot inside the collar of a white dress shirt, with dark trousers and highly-polished black shoes. Mother recognized him immediately. He was a popular radio personality in the NY-NJ broadcast area. They exchanged smiles and greetings. I noted only his mellifluous tones which were hypnotic. He had his butler get us two large, dense-pile white Turkish towels to help us dry ourselves.

As my mother explained about the tree, he issued orders for some number of people, who never showed themselves to us, to get chains and a vehicle to pull the barrier off the road. In the meantime he offered us tea. He ordered Earl Grey and finger sandwiches. Still dripping and creating a puddle, I scanned the spacious foyer. Overhead was a large but subdued crystal chandelier. Beyond us straight ahead, and down two broad steps, was a grand, mahogany-paneled room. On the left it had built-in bookcases filled with hundreds of leather-bound volumes, with titles embossed in gold.

Straight ahead at the end of the room there stood a huge flickering marble fireplace. Silver and gold awards of some kind adorned its ornately carved mantelpiece. Over it hung a large oil painting in a wide gold frame of a handsome black horse. I wondered if it was a race horse that he owned. I didn't ask but wanted to. I wish I had.

The fire's golden light warmed the large colorful Persian rug on which were stylishly scattered three stuffed mahogany chairs and a settee. On them was what I later identified as a likely historic William Morris fabric. There were three mahogany side tables, Tiffany lamps, and *objet d'art*. On the right-hand wall were what might have been oil masterpieces. Near the tall, dark-green draped window also on the right was a baby grand piano. I had never seen anything quite like this room before. Perhaps with the exception of a 1940's black-and-white British movie about someone's fine estate.

When the butler brought tea, the tea service was silver. It was brought on its large, matching tray. On it were thin, gold-rimmed bone China cups and saucers, linen napkins, matching dessert plates, fresh lemon wedges, milk in a silver creamer, sugar cubes with ornate silver sugar tongs, and monogrammed silver teaspoons. The cucumber and watercress finger sandwiches arrived separately on a three-tiered silver server with petit fours on the bottom tier. I was impressed at such an elegant repast, especially for two sodden strangers. Too bad I had stuffed myself on the hill. Now I wasn't all that hungry. To be polite I drank and nibbled and made what I thought were appropriately gracious sounds.

Sitting on our towels so as not to damage the museum-quality-looking furniture, I was enjoying this leisurely British tea. How much more sophisticated could I get than this? The broadcaster was asking my mother about what she did and liked. She shared her living on the Ladd estate and her love of plants. When she mentioned her love affair with Princess, he became more attentive. That piqued his interest. They quickly became engrossed in horse talk, laughing occasionally, their heads close together. While they chatted, I wandered around, exploring. I was afraid to touch anything in this beautiful museum but examined things closely.

By the time our host received news that the tree had been removed, it seemed like only a few minutes had passed. I was reluctant to leave. The radio celebrity who had talked animatedly with my mother during tea now held my mother's hand a heartbeat longer than a normal handshake. He looked into her eyes and smiled broadly. I sighed to myself. I could hear the violins well up in the background. It would have made such a romantic movie ... maybe like a "Brief Encounter" or "Casablanca."

Having no further storm-related problems, we arrived home safely, being only a little damp. We met my father at the door. He had only just arrived as well. My mother told my father what had happened. He became incensed. I didn't know why she had told him. I didn't see any reason to do so. We weren't late. He was not worried about us.

But suddenly he claimed my mother should have called him so *he* could have come to collect us. I wasn't quite sure how he would have done that. He didn't have a phone in the car. He didn't have a chain to move that massive tree trunk. Was he going to have us climb over it to whisk us away in his car, leaving the Model-A behind? I suspected he was jealous of the well-to-do celebrity and of his helping my mother ... and me.

When I looked at my mother questioningly, she covertly shared a mysterious cat-like "I've just had my cream" smile. That whispered to me she was very glad she hadn't called my father. She also wanted to let him know. That was the first flash of marital independence I had seen in her with him. That adventure had made the ordinary *extraordinary*. It had given her a sense of power. It was clearly well worth her putting up with my father's expected and forgettable anger. It had been like a fairy tale ... or something out of "Pride and Prejudice" or "Wuthering Heights." Just thinking about it made me smile and sigh again. I knew my mother would keep that flame alive too.

While we lived at Maple Cottage, my father thought it would be "fun," he said, for Wally and me to have sheep. I have no idea why he really decided on their purchase. My love of animals extended to all kinds, but why sheep? Again, I suspected it wasn't for us. My mother had objected. She was over-ruled. He bought two young sheep, which were no longer lambs. He then constructed a wood shed for them and an eight-by-eight pen of chicken wire. I named mine "Honey Lamb" and Wally named his "Sugar Lamb."

I fed them religiously. Putting leather dog collars on them to which I attached a heavy jute twine, Wally and I led them around the property. I tried to brush their tangled cream-colored wool to help keep them clean. And every morning in the winter I replaced their frozen water with fresh water. But despite everything I did, they sickened and died.

It turned out that in his impulsivity to get the sheep, my father had not learned anything about what was required to raise them. It wasn't that you just give them sheep food pellets, water, and a place to stay. He didn't even know he had to move their pen frequently. If not, the ground would become littered with their dropping. Further, they would not always have fresh grass to eat. That seemed so commonsensical to me, at least after the fact. The poor critters didn't stand a chance.

It seemed to me animals were constantly passing through our lives. They weren't shuffling slowly through. Instead they were speeding through on streamliner trains. Since these trains never slowed coming into a station, not one of the animals was to be with us for very long. As much as I loved animals, respected and enjoyed them, I would have preferred not to have had any. They resided with us for such a short time. They were being cavalierly given and taken away. That seemed so careless and heartless. It wasn't fair to them or to anyone else.

As per usual, I didn't say anything to that effect. I was still afraid to speak up. My mother told my father she didn't want any more animals. Her voicing her opinion had no effect on him. He always ignored her opinion. My K.H., however, would have firmly demanded he get no more animals, even those that normally only lived in the house. But even that wouldn't have helped as we continued to find out.

CHAPTER 17

Still Expecting Change

All this time I was still trying to get my father to accept me as me. The underlying problem was that once I started to try to gain his unconditional positive regard, I tended to keep on trying, and trying, and trying. Endlessly I was doing the same thing over and over again. Maybe it's a universal. All I knew was that I felt as though I *had* to. It didn't matter whether or not he had ever demonstrated any caring for me. It didn't matter if I had perceived it or just pretended I had. Before I was seven, I assumed he cared. That was enough. That was what I needed to recapture. I would go after that feeling with everything I had to get it.

That assumption had hooked me. Like a junkie, I kept trying to re-experience that elusive early "high." But the problem was I never could. There was no way I could, no matter what I did. I felt compelled to keep trying. Something *might* change, I kept telling myself. Irrationally, I was stuck.

With a gaping hole in myself I didn't want to give up. Maybe my father felt that way about his father too. There were hints of moments when he seemed so sad. As a child, I thought that was so but could never tell for sure. As I grew older, I suspected he had suffered the same fate he had visited upon me just in different sheep's clothing.

My grandfather did not make it easy to love him—he made it impossible. He was the type of father who held out his arms to his child who was standing on a wall and said, "Jump. I'll catch you. I promise I'll catch you. Go ahead, jump into my arms." And the moment the child jumped, he pulled his arms away, saying, "That will teach you not to trust what people say."

Maybe my grandfather didn't care if anyone loved him. All signs seemed to point to it. Besides, why would he? As I later thought, his children seemed to exist for one purpose—and one purpose only. They were to keep his name alive in perpetuity. But, perhaps more importantly, they were to satisfy his desire to move human chess pieces around. He was surely expert at doing that. Despite all the control, self-confidence, and assertiveness he had, that I didn't, I could never respect him. I wondered if my father respected him. Everything my father did seemed predicated on his father's questionable acceptance of his son.

It was time to move again which saddened me. With a van line behind us, we drove all the way to St. Petersburg Beach, Florida. This time we were without any animals. I can't say for sure what my father was doing for work at that time. I do know we were suddenly spending lots of money. Never going out to eat before, we began dining often at the fancy Imperial House restaurant that was part of the beach apartment complex where we now resided.

I suspected that much of the money was a result of all our furniture. The furniture had moved with us and was now being auctioned off after we arrived. Years later I puzzled about spending big bucks to move a van load of furniture to then auction it off. I wondered if my father had done a cost-benefit analysis before the move.

Late one morning I accompanied my father to the huge steel, hanger-like auction facility to speak with those who were handling our property. I felt like crying as I thought about all of our possessions being handled and bought by strangers. At least I still had my stuffed khaki-colored horse with the red string mane and tail and my black and gray mohair lamb. I had had them both since I was four. I no longer had the doll Mimi had bought for me. I no longer had all of my classics books series, with *Last of the Mohicans* and *A Tale of Two Cities*. I did manage to save a few as well as my *Wizard of Oz* series in its entirety.

For our auctioned-off life we had gotten a furnished apartment with maid service right on the beach. My parents bought a second-hand plane, a red and cream Piper Cub Super Cruiser, to refurbish. I still had my keyed clamp-on roller skates but that was all. My childhood was disappearing along with my possessions. But it seemed as if our financial yo-yo had rolled back up the string again.

To my mother's elation she and my father both began taking flying lessons. Having their plane at the small Pinellas County Airport gave them a chance to enthusiastically enjoy the airplane owner's culture there. My mother was at the hangar where they housed our plane nearly every day. While I was at school, she cleaned and waxed our plane's fabric surface making it shine. With her hair in short braids, in rolled up sleeves, jeans, and sneakers, she looked like a sun-kissed teenager sprucing up her first car. I hadn't seen her that cheerful in years. That is, except for the "magical" felled tree incident.

My mother took to flying like an eaglet. She had a deft touch with the control stick, rudder and elevator pedals. She could make the plane do nearly anything she wanted as she gained confidence. She and the plane were one. My father, on the other hand, had to feel in physical control every second. Rather than letting himself respond naturally to the plane's movement, he constantly ignored his feelings and intuition. He kept adjusting the controls to make the plane do his bidding, perhaps to create some sense of perfection.

When my mother finally soloed, she was ecstatic. She flew overhead, confidently rolled her wings at us, and circled the field. She lined up with her runway, flew into the wind, and then cut the throttle. Floating like a feather onto the pavement, she made a perfect three-point landing. I caught it on film. Later I had the clear, split-second shot framed for her. Her performance upset my father considerably.

When he soloed, he didn't bother rolling his wings at us. Instead, he likewise circled, lined up with his runway, and flew into the wind. But he misjudged his rate of descent. He was coming in too steeply and too fast. As he hit the runway, he hit nose first. He broke the wooden propeller on his landing, totally ripping off one of the blades. I suspected his high level of competitiveness with my mother had negatively influenced his performance. Flashing away the moment he touched down, I caught his ignominious approach on film. He destroyed the photo of his landing.

While my mother was jubilant beyond measure with her accomplishment, my father was vexed and humiliated. A woman, especially his wife, had bested him. He then tried hard to find ways to diminish what she had done. Simultaneously, he tried to elevate himself above breaking his propeller. This, however, only made him look foolish to anyone at the airport who heard him and had witnessed what he had done. All his excuses could never quite make it come out all right in the end. He'd have to live with the reality of it. But it chafed.

My mother kept her gleefulness secret. She alluded to it often but never in my father's hearing, "On my first try I floated just as easy as you please, making a perfect three-point landing. I thought your father would have a fit!" she laughed. It gave her a freedom, confidence, and achievement she had never before experienced. She had no intention of ever letting it go, even if only in her memory. Repeatedly over the years she showed me her pilot's license, wings, and AOPA, Aircraft Owners and Pilots Association, card.

It was good that she had it so firmly implanted in her recollection because she would never take to the air herself again. Things were about to change … once more. When that would happen, she would try to keep her sense of loss under wraps. Expressing it was useless and maybe even dangerous.

But she would truly miss flying and the airport camaraderie. She already had made plans for her first independent trip, to Sarasota and the Ringling Museum. She had met millionaire airplane owners and exchanged flying stories. She had laughed with them as an equal. She had thoroughly enjoyed it when then Yankees' owner Dan Topping prepared homemade chili on the tarmac for the gang at the hangar. This was a companionable life she had never known before. She would be desolate to be leaving it behind.

Before we left living on the beach, there was an increasing emphasis on my being a model little girl, maybe like a "daddy's little girl," but in name only. I didn't understand this sudden shift. I didn't necessarily have to be attired in dresses all the time. But my father expected me to act with feminine propriety every moment. I'm not sure I totally understood that considering how he said he felt about me.

There were no more tank tops. If a male stepped out of line, I was to respond appropriately. Or, at least, that's how I interpreted the "traditional female behavior guidelines" that he imparted to me. He did it somewhat indirectly by telling me what I shouldn't do.

Still that chubby child, I had what almost looked like breasts. However, my secondary sex-characteristic-producing hormones were not to kick into action for a few years. At one point I asked my mother if I could wear one of her satiny bras. It's not as though I could actually pour anything into her cup-size which was on the small side given her sylphlike figure. But I was feeling uncomfortable wearing even larger t-shirts with these two somewhat-pointy bumps beginning to show. Feeling a little freakish, I was concerned everyone was looking at me and chuckling to themselves.

At one point my mother took me to a doctor about my weight. I was only slightly overweight but I guess she was concerned. I had no idea if my father had put her up to it. Always fighting his own weight problem, he had a lustful relationship with food. He attacked it as if he were deprived and starving. He would scrape his ice cream dishes until you expected the glaze to peel off with the last molecules of cream and sugar.

I wasn't that food-oriented. I did, however, eat the popsicles and ice cream which he always brought home and had frequently. He never referred to my weight. Instead, he referred to my height, calling me "pygmy." I hated that. Even when I asked him not to, he chose not to stop because he thought it was funny.

After the doctor and my mother talked, he said to me, "If you want to have a boyfriend, you have to lose weight. You want to have a boyfriend, don't you?" I just looked at him. He was letting me know that in order to appeal to the opposite sex, I had to meet some standard body specifications which I obviously didn't. He was letting me know I wasn't acceptable as I was.

That seemed like a terrible thing to say to a child, even though I'm sure he meant it to be an encouragement. But I didn't feel encouraged by it. I felt that was simply another black mark against me. Besides, I wasn't particularly interested in boys at that time.

One afternoon I was sitting on the dark-green-painted wooden bench under a group of shadowing pines. They made a cool swishing sound in the breeze off the water. This was just across the street from our apartment. As I sat there quietly, I watched the ocean roll in, create foaming bubbles, and pull itself back out again. I was feeling the distant roar of thousands of miles of waves at the horizon. With me was *Treasure Island* which I had saved from the auction block. I read a lot and enjoyed living different lives, being someone else.

While I was engrossed in Chapter 3, a young boy, maybe my age, from the apartment complex came over to me. Wanting to play, he said silly things and asked lots of questions. "Who are you? Are you from around here? You don't look like any girls I know. Where do you live? Over there?" pointing. "How long have you lived here? My parents said your parents fly planes. Do you fly planes too? I'd like to fly like a bird. Would you like to be a sea gull? What are you reading? A comic book? No, *Treasure Island*? You want to be a pirate? I could be a pirate. Aaaargh," he tried to growl like Robert Newton in the Disney movie of "Treasure Island." "Are you going to be looking for buried treasure? I'd like to look for buried treasure."

He leaned over and tried to grab my book to run off with it to make me chase him. He was like a puppy that hadn't yet found a slipper to chew on and so was nipping at my ankles.

I tried to ignore him and continue reading but he kept fooling round. He wouldn't stop. "Go away." I said. "I'm busy. I want to read." I made a dismissive hand gesture. "Go home or play in the sand." I pointed at the water. "Go for a swim. Or take a long walk off a short pier (something I had recently heard and thought was terribly clever). Just leave me alone." If *this* was what I was supposed to lose weight for, the doctor was way off base. He'd have to find a more convincing line of persuasion. I definitely did not have much use for boys if this boy was representative. This one was acting like a jerk.

After a few more minutes of his ceaseless activity, he tried another tack. He walked behind me, stood quietly, leaned over my right shoulder, and looked down the front of my open-necked cotton blouse. Speaking loudly, he said, "I can see your boobies!" My reaction was immediate. As a "lady who had been accosted and insulted," I did what I thought I was supposed to do. I rose and slapped him across the face, as in some Victorian melodrama, but without the "Take that, you cad!"

As if struck by lightning, he stood stationary for a moment. His eyes and mouth wide open. Slowly he regained his senses. A pink splotch decorated his cheek where my open palm had connected with his face. Starting to bawl, he ran away home crying loudly. "Serves him right, the little creep," I mumbled. I thought no more about it except that I was proud I'd defended my honor and the "flower of maidenhood" everywhere. Overjoyed by my accomplishment, I eagerly went back to reading about Jim Hawkins, Long John Silver, Billy Bones, and their challenges.

But no sooner had I arrived back at our apartment than things abruptly changed. My father swooped in on me as I had barely opened the door. He demanded to know why I had done such a horrible thing. I stood there, brow furrowed, trying to get my bearings. What was he talking about? It suddenly became apparent. The boy had squealed to his parents who then had tattled to my father. He stood towering over me, his face drained of all color.

Since we seemed to be constantly on the lam from non-payment of rent, my father was perhaps petrified that someone, like the boy's parents, might sue him. But this time it was different. It was worse because his "unacceptable" daughter had committed an "unjustified assault." I was totally confused. What was going on? The boy had acted sexually toward me. I re-acted as I thought I had been taught to, as I was expected to. Besides, what was the big deal? We were just young children.

Instantly my father's face changed from white to magenta as he grew increasingly furious with my actions. He began shouting at me, "How could you do such a thing? Did he touch you?" I shook my head. "NO! Then why did you slap him?" He didn't give me a chance to answer. "Do you know the position you've put me in?!"

What position? I was taken aback, even more confused. I brought myself up with a start. Wait a minute! Why had my father not even for an instant thought that maybe things hadn't happened as he had heard? That maybe I had been in the right? That maybe it was the boy's fault? That maybe the boy deserved it ... and more ... for "molesting" his daughter?

I raised my eyebrows. He hadn't asked *my* side: What exactly had I done? How did I do it? Why had I felt it appropriate to do it? Everything was predicated on what the boy had told his parents and what his parents had told my father. Maybe there was a lot of

Signe A. Dayhoff, PhD

exaggeration and bias in their tales. I was appalled that he *never* defended me. Why was I automatically in the wrong? I tried to speak to attempt to get some clarification but was drowned out by my father's ranting.

My K.H. would have pressed harder, spoken louder, defended herself, and pointed out the injustice—whether or not it would have done any good. At least she would have made herself heard. If I had done that, my father would likely have considered it "sassing him." He would have punished me for that too, probably physically as he was wont to do.

After my one attempt, I was speechless. I shook my head in bewildered disappointment. I thought your family was supposed to be on your side. I thought they were supposed to, at the very least, *listen* to your side—certainly before judging you, pronouncing you guilty, and executing you. Apparently this was not the case in my "family." My mother had never uttered a word during my interrogation. But, sadly, I hadn't expected her too. The final verdict of my father's inquisitional court was that I had to go to talk to the boy and his parents ... and apologize. Apologize? *Me* apologize?!

To my mind that kid was the one acting like some pervert. How come I got the grief? His parents ought to have given him a swift swat on his backside for what he had done. I knew he hadn't told them what he had done. I was sure he had given them a sad tale of woe about this mean, evil girl who had just decked him with a sucker punch when he was standing around, doing nothing. Me apologize?

The little beast wasn't damaged. I hadn't blackened his eye, loosened any teeth, or even left a hand print. Although later on, I almost wished I had done at least one of those. I thought self-righteously that since this kid had already gotten away with it once, he would probably grow up to be a Peeping Tom, or worse. And I hoped with all my heart he would do it again. But this time he would really get slugged for his efforts, with no parents around to run crying to, to protect him. That was such a satisfying image ... but ... I still had to go apologize.

Then something delightfully surprising happened. One evening we all bundled into the car to go to the nearby drive-in theater. There was a double-feature but what caught my interest was "Pat and Mike" with Katharine Hepburn and Spencer Tracey which came on first. While a comedy, its main character was mesmerizing. The K.H. character, "Pat Pemberton," was a brilliant all-round athlete. She was a champion in golf and tennis who was creating a sensation nationally. She was strong, assertive, and purposeful except when her domineering fiancé was around. He wanted them to marry and for her to forget all about her athletic activities, "this nonsense" as he put it. His presence flustered her performance and made her doubt her confidence and competence.

The parallels to my life were obvious. But she could not and would not give up so easily. I loved it. This was definitely like my image of my K.H. But, alas, it was nothing like my image of me.

She was larger than life, behaving with the attitude I wanted so badly. Yet she was vulnerable to someone close to her who discounted and dismissed her accomplishments. She stood up for what she believed. She acted on her convictions. And she didn't have to be male to do it. That was my K.H. all over. This characterization made an indelible impression on me.

Shortly following that on-screen K.H. discovery, I was at recess at the Pinellas Elementary School when twin classmates approached me. They invited me to their upcoming birthday party. It appeared that everyone in our class had been asked. I was surprised I had been asked but very pleased. I couldn't wait to attend—it was acceptance of a sort. Then I saw Ruthie, a somewhat shy girl who blended in with the woodwork. She was often separate from the other students. I liked her and talked with her a lot. We seemed to have a lot in common. I hoped my friendship would help her leave her shell behind to some degree.

I sought out Ruthie. Not thinking about the remote possibility of selective invitations, I asked her if I'd see her at the party. I simply assumed I would and used the question to start a conversation. But to my horror and embarrassment, she told me she hadn't been invited. My face flushed. I was furious with myself for having asked the question and humiliating Ruthie. I was angry with the twins for having left her out.

I excused myself from Ruthie to find one of the twins. Shaking myself free of my embarrassment, I asked her point blank with an edge to my voice, "Why didn't you invite Ruthie? You've invited everyone else. How can you exclude her? That's not right. That's not fair."

Forthrightly she explained, "We didn't want her there"

Taking a slightly different tack, I nicely asked, "But would you consider changing your mind so she isn't the only one not invited?"

"No." It was obvious she had her own K.H. standing with her on this.

So taking on a Katharine Hepburn imitation, I stated somewhat brashly, "If you don't invite Ruthie to your party too, I'm not coming." It was as if my presence would hold a lot of social weight for her and force her to change her mind. That was a chuckle.

It didn't. They didn't invite Ruthie ... and I didn't go. While Ruthie and I tried to find something else to do together that Saturday by ourselves, neither one of us had transportation to do it. Complicating it, my father had expected me to go to this party. When I didn't, he questioned me. "You were so looking forward to going to this party. Why aren't you going? What happened to change your mind?"

Still not having gotten the message about keeping my thoughts to myself, I said, "They invited everyone but Ruthie. I said I wouldn't go unless they invited her too."

He raised his eyebrows dramatically as if to say he couldn't believe I had done such an incomprehensible thing. He said, "You did what? That was their party to invite whom they pleased. You had *no right*—no right at all—to demand that they invite someone else. I can't believe you. That was so rude. I can't imagine what you were thinking to act like that! How could you ... *my* daughter ... have done such an awful thing? You are such a disappointment."

Despite his outrage at my unacceptably "disgraceful" actions, I still felt righteous in my having stood up for Ruthie. Maybe it wasn't the polite thing to do. But I felt Ruthie deserved a "Pat Pemberton" in her corner fighting for her. At that fleeting moment, I was it.

My mother's birthday was arriving soon and I had only twenty-one cents to get her a present. Money was becoming scarcer so asking my father for some was not an option. I stopped at a small variety store just two blocks over to see what they had. They had some of the beautiful cobalt blue, flattened half-globe bottles with tall silver caps and dark blue lettering on a silver square saying "Evening in Paris." I had no idea how the toilette water smelled but they looked so elegant to me. But I couldn't swing the purchase. I was examining everything I could find.

When I came upon some small gray plastic viewers on snap key chains, I held one up to the light. In it I saw a photograph of a woman leaning forward cupping her face in her hands. She had a large bare breast which was hung over a piece of polished wood. As I was contemplating what it was supposed to mean, the store owner came over and gently took it from my hand. He asked, "What are you looking for?"

Explaining my predicament, I said, "It's my mom's birthday and I want to get her a gift." Then I asked, "Do you have anything I can give her for twenty-one cents?" He raised his hand to his chin as if massaging it. Minutes passed. It was soon obvious that he was having considerable difficulty thinking of anything.

So together we walked around the entire store, looking at the shelves. There was nothing. Everything was either too expensive or not suitable, like a can of Ajax Cleanser or rolls of toilet paper. I was so discouraged. Ten minutes later I as I sadly shuffled toward the front door, I spotted a tiny green plant in a two-inch-square pot without a label. "Hey! What about this?" I asked expectantly, my mood perking up.

"Well ...," he replied, "why ... yes. As a matter of fact, that's exactly 21 cents with the sales tax. I forgot all about that. That's a very good choice. I'm sure she'll like it."

"Yes, I know she will," I replied. "She loves plants."

He smiled as I clutched this miniature whatever it was in my hand. I was feeling on top of the world. I had found the perfect gift for her. It was only later that I realized how kind the proprietor had been to this fervent child who wanted so badly to please her mother with something special.

CHAPTER 18

Mooching Off Relatives

Our Florida stay was short-lived. We ultimately ran out of money, sold the plane, and hopped a heatless, foodless, shuddering ancient DC-3 to go to live with relatives. This was one more arrow in my father's dying sense of self-worth. We began taking advantage of two families of relatives, starting in Peapack-Gladstone with Uncle Dennis and Aunt Rachel. The embarrassment for my mother was palpable. She did all she could to help my aunt with chores and cooking. Her goal was to make all of us as invisible as possible. But this was impossible since we were significantly intruding on their space and lives, creating undeserved stress for them.

When Wally developed poison ivy blisters *all* over his body from playing outside, it became even more difficult. His eyes were swollen shut. Every movement prompted painful itching. He screamed as if being burned at the stake when he tried to urinate. My mother spent most of her time applying Calamine Lotion to his every square inch of his skin. She lay wet, cooling cloths on his skin creases so they wouldn't crack and possibly promote a secondary infection. This was in addition to trying to keep from contaminating any of the rest of us with anything that touched him.

My aunt and uncle had a swing set toward the back boundary of their rolling property. It was located on the only usable flat spot except for their small front yard. Between their property and the one behind it was a weather-beaten gray fence belonging to the back property. In that yard was a previously-paint-peeling ramshackle house with falling-down wooden sheds for animals. I couldn't see any grass but spied lots of mud. It made me think of penned up cows at some factory farm who stood in mud and feces until their hooves rotted away. I always worried about animals. But I didn't see any animals here.

As I played with the swing set's small trapeze one afternoon, a heavy-set, balding, middle-aged man in faded blue bib overalls sidled up to the fence and leaned over it. He reminded me of a "hillbilly" character from a "Ma and Pa Kettle" movie. I didn't know people really looked like that. I was swinging back and forth, hanging by my knees. I turned over through my arms to land on the ground, then jumped backward through my arms again. I was pretending to be a circus performer. High above the center ring, I was dazzling the awestruck audience on the bleachers below with my daring and dexterity.

I didn't like his leaning over the fence near me, watching me intently. But I wasn't within his arm's reach. As a result, I didn't focus too much on him at that moment. I wasn't going to let him spoil my fun. There seemed so little of it these days.

Before long he spoke to me. He introduced himself, "I'm Mr. Plummerstadt." Then he started asking me questions, "Who are you? Where do you live? In the white house up there?" He pointed back up the yard. I didn't tell him anything. I didn't like his smirking smile which revealed brown-mottled and absent teeth. I had never seen anyone with teeth like that before. Didn't he brush his teeth? I wanted him to go away. I wanted him to leave me alone to wow the crowds. I kept ignoring him as I swung on the trapeze.

He didn't take a hint. Then he changed the subject of his running monologue to kittens. He caught my attention as he began telling me about his having kittens. "This cat that hangs around had kittens in my shed over there." He pointed to a dilapidated wooden enclosure. "What was I going to do with kittens? They make a lot of noise and are very demanding. So I kicked the mother cat off my property. Then I drowned them kittens in a bucket of water. That's the bucket over there." He pointed to an old dented pail. "You should have seen them kittens struggle and scream for their mom. Took me a while to hold them all down until they all stopped struggling."

What? What was he saying? I looked at him hard. Was this supposed to be funny? It certainly wasn't. Was he trying to scare me with this kitten horror story? He was definitely doing that. He knew he had my attention. He went on, telling more about the horrific process as my eyes widened. He detailed how he had to keep them from treading water and trying to crawl up the slippery side of the galvanized bucket in order to survive. How they kept bobbing to the surface again and again until he was sure he'd filled their little lungs with water. I was disgusted but mesmerized by this atrocity. It was so grotesque I couldn't believe it—I didn't want to believe it. Did people really do such unspeakable things? When I observed his self-satisfied smile, my heart stopped. I knew he wasn't kidding.

I was torn. I didn't want to let him scare me away. I wanted to play for a while longer. But he was a murderer. He killed kittens and he enjoyed it. He bragged about it. He was too creepy to stay around. As I hung by my knees for the last time, he leaned farther over the fence. Looking around, as if checking for eavesdroppers, he provided me with a wide, toothy grin. Then he whispered, as if confiding a secret to me, "Gentlemen like to look at little girls' panties." Up to that moment, I had not given my clothing a thought. As I innocently hung by my knees, I was exposing my underpants. Though I didn't know anything about "dirty old men," he had set off my full-bodied panic alarm. I had to get away from him immediately!

My K.H. would have told him straight out, "I'm going to call the police if you don't stop bothering me," would have played a little longer, this time without revealing underwear, than strolled off, not to give him the satisfaction of her running away. But I wasn't that cool and collected. I jumped down, charging back, as if the devil were chasing me, to tell my aunt.

But to my great surprise, she didn't say anything. Didn't she hear me? Didn't she understand? Didn't she believe me? What was going on? It was as if I hadn't told her something important. I was confused. She didn't do anything so far as I could tell. I know she didn't tell my father or mother. Because I was scared, I never played on the swing set again. I hoped my younger female cousin, Deidra, didn't either, even if she were totally covered, when that "person" was around.

Immediately after that, I had a recurring nightmare. Mr. Plummerstadt was there, larger than life, drowning kittens in slow motion. I was screaming for him to stop as I struggled to grab and overturn the bucket. The kittens' high-pitched mews of panic were spurring me on to try to rescue them somehow. He was laughing at me, now putting his hands all over me. I knew he was going to hurt me, like the kittens. Suddenly I saw well-dressed men (his so-called "gentlemen") gathering all around me, moving in close, trying to look at my panties. Screaming, I'd awaken in a sweat. My heart was tripping as I gasped for breath. Scanning the room, I quickly checked to make sure no one was there trying to disrobe me with their eyes or their hands.

From then on I became very conscious about being adequately covered. I tended to assess all men I saw with wariness. Moreover I felt prohibited from doing fun things I had done before. I had to make sure that I didn't do anything to risk a repetition of the Plummerstadt incident. Somehow I knew down deep, even though I could not yet understand the full implications of his behavior, that I had been very lucky that my encounter with real "evil" wasn't more than it was.

During that time, my father's creativity and motivation peaked again so he studied the classifieds in the *New York Times.* Circling possibilities, he spent time on the phone arranging appointments. Then with great purpose he took the train to New York City to interview for jobs. This was in spite of my cousins' cat, Mr. Betsy. Originally thought of as a female only to be discovered to be a male, Mr. Betsy had been displaced from his regular sleeping quarters in my aunt and uncle's bedroom when my mother and father took it over. Disgruntled, he decided to show his displeasure. He urinated in my father's dress shoes which were on the floor in their clothes closet.

As much as I hated everything associated with my father and our ongoing state of adversity, I had to empathize with him on this hot, humid mid-July day as he rode the train to Manhattan. With this newly discovered acrid scent wafting around him, he was sending fellow travelers scurrying for distant seats. It accompanied him to each of his interviews. There's no doubt he made quite an impression on those job decision makers.

Because he seemed deathly afraid of negative evaluation, this situation must have been like putting his head down over the basket to catch it when the guillotine blade fell to cleave his head from his shoulders. He was trying so hard this time that the cat piss situation didn't seem quite fair. When he didn't get any of the jobs he sought, he must have thought that life was merely lifting its leg on him ... again.

CHAPTER 19

Bearing My Pre-Teens

After staying with my aunt and uncle for months and months, we moved to Point Pleasant, New Jersey, into a rented house on River Road. This was a dead end street just above the canal which bisected the town from the Manasquan River Inlet to Barnegat Bay. Here I attended fifth and sixth grades. I made friends. And I started reading "Nancy Drew" mysteries by Carolyn Keene. As much as I loved them and read them quickly, I could buy them only infrequently. Nancy was like my teenage K.H., doing what she needed to do to uncover secrets and solve mysteries. She was outspoken. She stood on her own, with agility of mind and body. She would do what she needed to do. That's what I was going to do, as soon as I figured out how to start.

When my mother could drive me to school before my father left for work, she did. But I frequently had to walk the several miles home. One time it had rained in the morning so I had worn red, heavy rubber boots to school. During the day I hid them under my desk because I had no place else to store them. Wearing them all day would not have been "fashionable."

As the bell rang, declaring the end of the school day, I found the weather had cleared and the sun was shining brightly. It was now warm outside. I didn't have a ride back home. Wearing my raincoat, a gift from my Aunt Mona, Uncle Barry's wife, and with an armload of books to carry, I had no room to carry my boots as well. This meant I had to put them back on to start my leisurely peregrination home. My feet started sweating.

If only I had a book bag to fling over my shoulder or strap on my back, I could carry the troublesome boots in it. I'd have to be sure to create something to carry my stuff in if I couldn't buy one. But for now, I would have to put the boots on again. I knew I'd look like a dodo as I clopped along the sidewalk in these gunboats without rain. Besides, my loafers were going to get all wet from condensation as well over the long walk home. What would that do to the leather?

Approaching Ocean Road, I suddenly had the need to go to the bathroom. I was experiencing cramping pain and pressure. My bladder was threatening me. Fearful I couldn't make it home in time, I tried to take my mind off it. I thought about the bicycle I had wanted forever but would never get. I thought about how I could be home in no time if I had one. I thought how I wouldn't be in this predicament if I had one.

Finally I turned right on Osborn Avenue, getting closer to River Road which was only two blocks to go. If only I could grab myself to mechanically hold back the flow, just in case. In polite society such maneuvers were simply not acceptable. But this was urgent, an impending emergency. My K.H. reminded me, "You have to do what you have to do. You can't be so concerned about the evaluations of others." But, since I really needed both hands for my pile of books, it really didn't matter whether I'd look as if I were playing with myself as I walked along. I turned the corner on River Road. I was getting closer. Maybe I was going to make it after all. I walked faster. That move turned out to be a bad idea.

To my utter humiliation, I traversed only as far as the rose arbor that covered the entrance to our walk to the front door. My body took over control of my bladder. It released my urinary sphincter. The deluge came. My underpants were soaked. My half-slip and straight rayon navy blue skirt were spotted. My knee socks were soggy. My boots were full of urine. Slowly sloshing to the side porch by the kitchen, I called to my mother. Miserably I informed her of my accident.

My mother carefully helped me slip off my boots, one at a time, as I stayed upright, balancing with one hand on her back. She emptied them in the toilet. Then she removed my shoes still mired in them. With dish washing liquid in the boots, she washed them out with the hose on the side of the house. They sat upside down on the porch to dry. Just inside the kitchen door she retrieved a towel to wrap around me. She then took my clothing to deposit in the washing machine and examined my shoes.

While my clothing could be washed to be good as new again, my shoes were another story. Sloshing in urine, they were likely to be less fortunate. She rinsed them off with the hose too. Then she stuffed them with newspaper to help hold their shape and put them too on the porch steps. However, shaking her head in dismay, she said, "You might as well be ready to say good-bye to them. We'll do what we can but I don't know if we can get rid of the urine smell. That's too bad." It was too bad. My Bass black loafers were my favorite shoes. I would be sad to see them go, but I couldn't repeat my father's urine-smelling shoes scenario.

That incident became our secret. My mother and I referred to it with a chuckle as the "Johnstown Flood." There was no reason to tell my father about it. He most assuredly would have seen it as another black mark against me. I was sure he would have chalked it up to my not being able to control my bladder, as he obviously did on long trips, and/or my not being smart enough to use the bathroom before leaving school. My having ruined a good pair of shoes in the process was totally unacceptable. My father was not a great believer in accidents. To him everything happened for a reason. The reason to his mind was generally human stupidity—in this case, *my* stupidity again.

In order to get that bicycle I now felt I truly needed, I had shoved my pride aside on two separate occasions to literally beg for one. I tried a cost-saving entreaty with my father since I thought it most likely would appeal to him, "I could go to the grocery store if I had one to get items we needed. That would save you on gas. It would be a shame to waste gas and your time when I could do it for you."

My father was adamant. "No." He cited safety reasons, "There's too much traffic. There are no traffic lights between here and Ocean Boulevard. There are no bicycle lanes. You'd have to ride on the sidewalks and that's illegal." Those arguments never seemed to have much validity since children bicycled all around us without incident.

"I'll watch for traffic and signal my turns. There's not much traffic between here and Ocean Boulevard."

"No," he replied and that was that. So I continued to wait silently, pining away for one.

Then something totally unanticipated happened to change that situation. For a Halloween party at the elementary school, my mother created a dazzling robot costume for my brother. The head and body were cardboard boxes covered in aluminum foil. With foil-wrapped spiraling wire she created flexible legs and arms. She gave him foil-covered shoe-box shoes then dressed the robot body with all sorts of wires, tubes, switches, and realistic-looking gadgets.

When given the opportunity to express it, she showed she was incredibly clever. Needless to say, Wally won first prize which, lo and behold, was a bicycle! Now what would my father do? Was he going to take away his son's beautiful silver Raleigh, the prize he had just won? My father could not do that to Wally. But, therein lay the problem. My brother was four years younger than I. What about my father's lame excuse for *my* not having a bicycle? He had quite a quandary to resolve and most certainly hated having to deal with it.

I did what my K.H. would have done. I had several debates with him about fairness. After those debates, I won. I loved my K.H. Now my father had to pony up for a Schwinn red-and-white girl's bike, equipped with a basket and a bell, for me. I always worried about expenses. I was as penny-pinching as possible. But this time I buried that concern and shoved it into my subconscious. I wanted that bicycle. And if my little brother could have one, I surely could too. Fair is fair. I justified my desire by reminding myself how hard I had been working at being a "good girl" and a good student, one of which he could be proud, if he were *ever* to be proud of me. I deserved it!

As the holidays rolled around, we needed decorations for our Christmas tree. My mother devised ways to have them by using construction paper, foil paper, newspaper, paint, glue, and glitter. Using fruit as *papier maché* forms, she taught us how to make colorful, sparkling balls to hang. With strips of construction paper, she wove three-dimensional German stars and dotted them with glitter too. As they turned with any motion of the air, they reflected the strings of red, blue, green, and yellow lights that lay on the tree branches. Together we made several twenty-foot colorful construction-paper chains, Santa mobiles, and yarn-wrapped pipe-cleaner Santa's elves and carolers. However, we no longer had any of her Christmas fireplace mantle scene. But at this house we didn't have a fireplace for it anyway.

And with the gold foil paper she cut large circles, cut radii toward the center, then rolled each section in to a cone shape. Clustering several of them together, she made a glorious sunburst for the top of the tree. This likewise would have been the crowning touch for the tree at Rockefeller Center. Years later I used these types of decorations on my trees and always adorned the top of the tree with this golden porcupine ball.

I'm sure my father who was a Christmas fanatic enjoyed the result. In that respect he was very child-like. But he never participated in the construction end of it. I'm not sure I ever heard him comment on those decorations. His participation was decorating the tree "properly" with the lights and accoutrements. Everything had to be just so.

He always took the lights as his own purview to place with calculated care. If you hung any balls and didn't put them, or any other decorations, in the "right" places, he would bring it to your attention or he would move them himself. While I could place stretched pieces of cotton on the branches to simulate snow, only he was allowed to hang the silver cellophane rain, piece by piece by piece, on the tree as the final act.

That was the Christmas he gave my brother and me an unwrapped, partially-open, twenty-two pound cardboard box for a gift. Inside were two kittens sitting in sand they were to use as their litter pan. We named them "Lucy" and "Desi." My mother had always claimed to "hate" cats. However, when I asked her directly about it, she admitted she never really had any acquaintance with one.

Ironically, before anyone knew it, she had become the light in their eyes—the only one who mattered in their feline world. They cuddled with her on the sofa, purring loudly. They slept with her every night in bed, under the covers at her feet. She was one of them and they were at one with her. It wasn't long before she was a cat lover supreme, and remained so. This was even when those two had hopped onto the stove top one evening during dinner and began orgiastic licking of what was left of pork chops and sauerkraut in the glass baking dish. She forgave them even when their intestines rebelled the next day against their having ingested the overly-rich snack.

After that Christmas my middle school was having free Friday night dances for the sixth graders in the gymnasium. This Friday the snow had been falling all day. It had been creating drifts for hours. The streets were nearly un-navigable with no snow plows in evidence. But I was desperate not to miss this night's dance. My father assured me the school would not have it because of the storm. But I couldn't be consoled. I was already dressed for the event. I was dying to be seen and dance. Fortunately by this time as I watched my ice cream intake, my extra weight had just slipped off me.

To my everlasting surprise, my father suddenly hustled me into my coat. In the car, we drove at five miles an hour through the still-banked streets. We reached the school some thirty minutes later. The school was indeed unapologetically completely dark. Acting unlike himself, my father never made a comment about it. I had no idea why on this particular night he gave in to my wishes. I found that confusing. Maybe he couldn't take my begging and pleading, which I loathed doing. But all he had to do was tell me to stop and he wouldn't have heard another word. Was it conceivable that he wanted to *please* me? I don't know. That seemed hard to believe. But there was something sweet about his risking an accident on icy streets to fulfill my wish. I thanked him. But in my heart I appreciated it more than he'd ever know.

Besides dances I could infrequently go to a Saturday movie. Movie tickets were only thirty cents at the time yet I often didn't have it. My father, however, always had his air-polluting cigarettes. Despite my rare attendance, it was in the local Point Pleasant movie theater that I received my first kiss, well, sort of. I had come to watch Elvis Presley in his first movie, "Love Me Tender." I can't say I had ever swooned over Elvis even when he gyrated his hips to Ed Sullivan's dismay on TV's "Toast of the Town." He sang ballads well and I liked his "Love Me Tender" version of "Aura Lee." But I hadn't come to see Elvis. I had come to see a movie, any movie, to get away, to escape into another world, any other world, for a while.

Some movies had stories that pulled you along, hypnotized. Some had stars that made you wish you had breasts, a waist, hips, and legs from here to there. Some were deceptive in a suspenseful but fun way, like the Saturday afternoon movie serials: "Flash Gordon" with Buster Crabbe, "Phantom Empire" with Gene Autry, and "Don Winslow of the Navy" with Don Terry. One week the hero was flying off a cliff in his runaway vehicle and the next, he was saved by an overhanging branch just *before* he reached the cliff edge. Not exactly honesty in advertising, but you gave them your willing suspension of disbelief and breathed a sigh of relief when the hero made it through another disaster.

Seated five rows back from the screen and Elvis, I was alone until a boy named Bill had slipped into the seat beside me. He was on my right in the scantily-occupied theater. It was obvious he did not have to sit by me. Even though he was my age, he had been tagged as having a "bad reputation," whatever that meant. I knew him only slightly. I had met him in the music store where my father worked. He was friends of the store owner's son. They played music together.

My mind was shooting in different directions. My groin was responding with warm, heavy tingling. Feeling excited in various parts of my body was a new sensation to me. What was my body telling me? What did his action mean? Did it mean he liked me?

Eating salty peanuts from a clear cellophane bag, he reeked of them. Fortunately, I liked peanuts enough that it wasn't repulsive. Slowly he moved closer to me. He quietly leaned over and kissed me. It landed gently on my cheek. It missed my mouth by two full inches. I couldn't tell if he intended to kiss my cheek or he was going for the gold and his aim was way off.

But it didn't matter. This was my first real kiss of any kind. His restrained behavior made me wonder how "bad" Bill could have been since he didn't try anything. He hadn't tried to put his arm around me. He hadn't tried to grope me in any way. He kissed me and left. Thank goodness. Any untoward touching would certainly have spoiled that sweet moment for me.

Despite his coating my cheek with a crust of sodium chloride, I enjoyed it. Then later, I worried endlessly about becoming "pregnant"! I knew this was unbelievably stupid. I already knew in detail how babies came to be. Yet, I continued to worry about it. Those burgeoning sexual feelings played with my emotions. When no baby bump appeared, I dropped the needless thought immediately. That was my first *conscious* excursion into how irrational thoughts could overpower you and hold you captive.

CHAPTER 20

Embarrassing Me Publicly

One afternoon in unalloyed happiness I saw my Uncle Barry, from Sherborn, Massachusetts, pull into our short un-paved drive. He had come to visit his brother. He was so young and handsome. His ready smile crinkled his robin's egg blue eyes so you knew he meant he was glad to see you. He was shorter and slimmer than my father. He was obviously in good shape, probably from having been in the Air Force. If only, I used to sigh, I had been older and he hadn't been married. Oh, well. It was better than having a crush on the oh-so-distant Cary Grant.

It was then I made a painfully critical error. I decided to hang around him while he was there. Hopefully not being too obvious as I mooned over him, I sat listening as he and my father talked in the backyard. They were standing in the pine needle-cover near the steps of our screened-in porch. I was quietly ensconced on a step next to my father. Without any notice, my father grabbed my right hand, pulling me to a standing position. He started telling my uncle how I embarrassed him by biting my nails. What? I gasped as my mouth fell open and my heart burst out of its starting gate.

He waved my hand around as he expressed his repulsion over what I'd done. He said, "I can't believe she has done this to herself. Her hands look so ugly. It's humiliating that she's a daughter of mine." Then he shoved my hand into my uncle's as if it were some vile inanimate object. He told him, "Look at what terrible things she's purposely done to herself. And, she keeps on doing it. It's disgusting."

Why was he being so cruel? Why trying to hurt me? I was mortified. Hey, I wanted to shout, I'm here! You're talking about me in front of me! Instead, I felt myself melting emotionally into a puddle like the Wicked Witch of the West.

My K.H. would have demanded they let go of her hand. Instead, squirming, I pleaded, "No. Please. No," I tried to get pull myself loose. I so wanted to be perfect in my uncle's eyes. I didn't want to be seen as some child who anxiously gnawed on her fingers, leaving short, sometimes jagged nails. I was being condemned for allegedly destroying the "grace and beauty" that my hands were supposed to display. I panicked. My heart was exploding. I felt like a captured animal, pinned in a steel-jawed trap. The teeth were cutting into my flesh. I knew I'd have to chew off that limb to escape. To my horror when I couldn't wriggle out of my uncle's grip, my panic hit over-drive. I did the only thing I could. I automatically kicked my uncle in the shins. He let go. I ran, sobbing, into the house.

What had I done? My favorite uncle! I'd acted like a crazy person. And then I couldn't bear to show my face to him before he left. I couldn't even apologize which I wanted desperately to do. I felt I had ruined everything. NO! NO! NO! I bellowed to myself. *My father* had ruined everything!

Full of humiliation and rage, I wanted to shout at my father, "How could you do such a horrible thing? Have you no decency? How could you embarrass me like that in front of *him*?" My K.H. would have expressed her anger openly. Unlike her, I screamed under my breath, "You sunovabeech bassted!" If I'd really said to him what I wanted to, I would have felt his belt on my legs again.

The next thing I knew, our television disappeared. Was it stolen? As my mother explained, my father had sold it to our oldest friends who happened to live two blocks from us. We needed the money to pay our rent. We'd known the Callahans since we'd lived in Florham Park and Madison, New Jersey, the first and second rented places I'd lived, not counting the hospital in Summit listed as where I was born. Their daughter, Maureen, and I had been friends from close to the beginning. Now she had both a fun, Romaine lettuce-eating dog, named "Gordo," and our television.

My mother and Henny, who was a whiz at making beautiful clothes for her daughter, were fast friends. So when Henny invited us over for dinner and to watch the Voice of Firestone on their "new"

TV, my mother was particularly embarrassed. They were being so kind and helpful to us in every way. Even after we lost the house on River Road, Henny and Clarence let us stay at their home for ten days as we packed our meager gear to ready us to move north again.

It was at this agonizing time at their home that I developed breast pain and cramps. To my surprise and dismay I had just begun to menstruate. My body couldn't have picked worse timing. I know I was supposed to be "happy" I was now "becoming a woman," but the pain I was experiencing was extreme. It was only a harbinger of things to come. My mother found me some Kotex. Perhaps if I had had a different relationship with my father, I might have shared this momentous change with him. But I thought he would dismiss it as unimportant. Or he would be embarrassed I had chosen to speak of it to him. Or he would use it as another thing to hold against me—now he *really* had to "worry" about me and boys.

As if a punishment from the forces of the universe, every month thereafter for decades I spent ten days in utter misery. Often doubled over in pain, I lay in bed in a fetal position hugging a heating pad to my lower abdomen when I could. I was bloated with nearly ten pounds of water-weight gain with diarrhea; enlarged, tender breasts; and flowing as if an artery had been punctured. Despite lots of precautions, like doubling my protection, I would have embarrassing accidents. These could occur anywhere at any time, over the years making me feel even more "unacceptable."

When it came time to make the move north, my father gave Lucy and Desi away. He said, "We can't take the cats with us because we don't know for sure where we we're going, but likely to your Uncle Barry's." I don't know if he knew it or didn't care that giving away Mother's cats was an especially deep loss for her. They shared their love with her unconditionally. She could talk to them and they listened. They were always mutually touching. Our animals were forever traveling through our lives, moved around a game board like checkers. They had no more security than we did, often being "abandoned" too when they were "inconvenient."

We made that move to Sherborn, likewise without our beloved bicycles, to take advantage of Uncle Barry, Aunt Mona, and my four cousins: Ronnie, Arnold, Carl, and Kristen. Time with them was very difficult because of the pressure it put on my aunt and mother. Their family tried their best to cope, but we just stayed and stayed. While there, I attended seventh and eighth grades at Pine Hill School. I made a fired clay head of one of our Great Danes for my mother, won a waltz contest at school, and helped start a group of cheerleaders that encouraged the eighth-grade boys' basketball team.

Before I began playing basketball in eighth grade, I had no idea I had a real breathing problem. But after ten strenuous minutes in one game when I ran offside to get the basketball, I discovered I couldn't breathe. I was gasping for breath. But my lungs weren't cooperating. The world was turning inky around me. I was feeling oddly cold. The floor was coming up to meet me. My body wanted to go into panic mode. I resisted, constraining myself to stay calm, long enough until I could recover.

This was the distress I had been experiencing in the presence of tobacco smoke, thanks to my father and his habit. But I still did not have a diagnostic label for my pulmonary problem. Making light of it, I didn't encourage my mother to seek one. We sought medical attention only in super-emergencies. Money was too tight. There was no such thing as health insurance.

Throughout my school years, we moved what seemed like all the time—at least every two years. My father continued to flit from job to job, making our financial security as stable as a Slinky cascading down the stairs. By the time we gave my aunt, uncle, and cousins their home back to move to Millis, Massachusetts, I had already been to twelve schools. Entering high school in Millis, I added number thirteen. This circumstance consigned me to always being the "new kid"—always being on the outside looking in.

CHAPTER 21

Stripping My Soul of Its Worth

Millis was a small town, south of Sherborn, based on a manufacturing economy. There was Cliquot Club sodas bottling plant which was famous for its ginger ale for eighty years and Ruberoid, one of the nation's largest manufacturers of asphalt and asbestos roofing materials and allied products. There was also Herman Shoe Company which had made boots for the military in the Spanish-American War and in World War II and the Causeway Street and the Brickyards for clay excavation and brick making.

Most of the students in the high school had grown up together. They had attended the same school in the same class since the first grade. As a result, they tended to be less accepting of strangers into their long-time closed circle. It was understandable but it didn't help me as I diligently tried to join in. Continually having to attempt to help people get to know me and like me was exhausting.

I was so tired of being the stranger among them. It didn't help that because I had moved around so much and experienced so much in my travels, I was a little more mature than some of my classmates. It likewise didn't help that it was senior, not freshman, males who were the ones paying attention to me in the halls before and between classes. At least that attention gave me hope I might fit in someplace well enough to be accepted.

After a particularly discouraging first four weeks of trying to hurry up the process of creating friendships, I did what I knew I should *not* do ... no matter what. It was dumb. I knew it was dumb. The result was a foregone conclusion. It was irrational. But I still felt compelled, like a piece of iron being drawn to a magnet, to do it. It was so completely against my better judgment. But, heaven help me, I did it anyway. I totally ignored my K.H.'s vehement rational protestations. Some people never seem to learn. At this time, sad to say, I was one of them.

Holding my breath, I asked my father why I was having difficulty becoming friends with my new classmates. I was like a puppy constantly being swatted with a newspaper for no observable reason but hoping that the next time things would be different—that, instead, I'd get a puppy biscuit, a pat on my head, or even a smile and soothing word, showing I was acceptable.

According to Albert Einstein, "Insanity is repeating the same mistakes and expecting different results." I was living proof of this. But I hated to give up the possibility that circumstances will somehow be different *this* time. I hated to give up the possibility that his attitude, mood, how he related to the subject matter, or some newly acquired sensitivity might be just enough to tip the balance positively in my favor.

I wanted to think he would feel flattered I sought out his advice. And, I certainly didn't want to think of my asking my father for help as a "gargantuan mistake." But I knew it was. My K.H. was still blistering my ears with, "NO! DON'T! You know what will happen. Things have NOT changed! Run, don't walk, to the nearest exit!"

My father sat me down on his and my mother's bed with its white chenille bedspread. Sam, our current Tabby cat, lay near the pillow, sucking on the fabric tufts and flexing his front paw claws in a state of kitten-like ecstasy. It was in cruel contrast to what was about to happen. In response to my cry for help, my father was prepared to share with me his wisdom from on high. He would tell me what the situation truly was and why it was that way. It soon became obvious that he felt he "knew" he had his fingers on the pulse of it. He knew precisely what I needed to know so I could straighten myself out in my ongoing, self-inflicted mess.

What could he have said to me? He could have said that I was at a disadvantage because I was new. I didn't have all their years of shared experiences and things in common with them. People, especially in small towns, tended to take longer to warm up to those who are new or a little different. He could have said it was *not* my fault. These things take time. I was eager to get the process rolling. If I kept on

116

being my friendly self and open to others, things would change for the better over time. But no, he took a different and predictable tack. And after all my fifteen years with him, I was still not prepared for it. While hope still sprung eternal, a premonition laid a cold finger on my heart.

Standing beside me, looking directly at me, he started by firing a mortar shell between my eyes, "You are super-critical of others. That's why you have no friends." I sat there numb, unbelieving. Then one by one he ticked off a long list of character flaws he ascribed to me: "selfish, self-centered, impatient, argumentative, stubborn, standoffish, arrogant, know-it-all, thoughtless, lacking respect ..." the list went on and on. Fortunately, at this time I was old enough to realize that all these deficiencies were, in fact, his own. He was projecting them onto me.

In retrospect, it was *almost* comical. For a while I had been using him as a negative role model. My hyper-awareness of his less desirable character traits had prompted me to try hard to recognize and counteract those traits whenever I found any semblance of them in myself. Over the years it had been too easy to unconsciously emulate him and internalize his behaviors. These were even those behaviors I found despicable. It was monkey see, monkey do. I had done the same thing with my mother. So "super-critical," I knew, wasn't describing me. I had been working my buns off to be sensitive to others, more objective, and definitely less judgmental than I, perhaps, might have been otherwise.

Of course, my K.H. would not have asked him in the first place. And in the second place if he had said those things to her, she would have disengaged herself emotionally. She would have said, "I do *not* accept your assessment of these things. I see it differently" Then she would have left him to puzzle over her "contrariness," the one fault he hadn't listed for me.

To him everyone was stupid and blame-worthy but him. He criticized everything and everyone constantly. Nothing was right or good enough. One time before this calculated demolition of my ego, I had asked him to read a class paper I had written carefully and was ready to turn in. The result was covered in blood from his negative comments. Ironically, when I revised it as precisely as he had suggested, he criticized the result even more. That was the last time I ever showed him any of my writing. If he thought he was being helpful to me, he was purposely deluding himself. In the future I would step back to be my own literary critic—but a constructive, not destructive, one.

One time he did get a much-deserved, albeit, momentary, comeuppance for his criticism of others. To my perverse delight I had the good fortune to witness it. Too bad it wasn't related to me, but. He had been watching the Boston talent show, "Star of the Day," and criticizing the performers for what they did or didn't do. Their voices were sharp, flat, or off-key. They were nervous or uncoordinated. They moved their lips when speaking for their ventriloquist's dummy. They had no grace, timing, or coordination when they danced.

The next contestant was a young girl who seemed a little awkward in her movements as she sang. I hadn't been paying close attention. It was difficult to do so over my father's streaming critiques. Her voice was good and I thought she was, perhaps, a little nervous. Performing in front of people can be anxiety-provoking even for well-known actors like Lawrence Olivier and singers like Barbra Streisand.

My brother, Wally, who had been watching the program more closely, had seen her walk onto the stage. Again my father started in, ragging on her mercilessly: she looked up all the time; she seemed somewhat jerky in her movements; her voice wasn't perfect. I kept thinking who appointed you the William Morris Talent Agency?

Finally Wally interrupted this tirade with a classic show-stopper. "What do you want?" he demanded of his father with more than a hint of sarcasm. "She's blind!"

My father quickly shut up. I clamped my hand firmly over my mouth and left the room speedily. I was about to explode with laughter all over him. I wanted to shout, "Go for it, Wally! I'm proud of you for standing up to him. That was very gratifying." If only there had been more of such instances, especially with me. Maybe then my father might have learned something from them. But, then again, in reality, I didn't really think it was likely—or even possible.

In addition to his criticizing everything, he also let it be known that it was likewise everyone else's fault his life had turned out as it had. He even accused my mother, brother, and me. "You are responsible for my life being such a mess. Having a wife and family has been a burden on me so enormous that it has doomed me to being a failure." It was clear he saw his life circling the toilet bowl, totally out of his control. He was, in essence, a marionette, controlled by others. He indicated we should feel guilty for having metaphorically slit open his carotid artery, drained all his blood, and then handed him a formaldehyde highball.

To hear him tell it, his life was the equivalent of a pile of chicken manure. He was being smothered and couldn't shovel his way out because it had been heaped on him so deeply. He never dared to consider the degree to which his own father had, in effect, dumped it on him starting early in his childhood. If such were the case, he had been wallowing in fowl feces well before we ever came on the scene. He just didn't want to know it. And he certainly couldn't see his own physical and psychological complicity in it.

That was an "aha!" *I* wasn't the *only* one who had made his life a living hell, a lingering disaster, a tragic disappointment! He had branded all of us with a scarlet "G" for" guilty" because the shame was ours. But the more I thought about it, the more I was convinced the "G" should have stood for "gutless." That would have been a more appropriate description. We allowed him to blame us without a single word of protest. I didn't say anything, depressingly as usual. But my K.H. would have stated, "I don't and won't accept blame for your life. It is yours to do with as you choose. If you didn't like any of your options early on, you could have chosen not to act on any of them. It's still your choice and your problem, not mine."

CHAPTER 22

Rescuing My Mother

As he finished his appraisal of me as a personal and interpersonal flop, I sat quietly. My ears were ringing. My blood pressure was skyrocketing. And tears were rolling down my flushed cheeks, dripping onto my white Oxford cloth long-sleeved blouse, pooling on my straight gray light-weight wool skirt, and dotting my black tights beneath. But as agonizing as that was, that was *the* two-by-four to the back of my skull that I truly needed.

Not that he was speaking one scintilla of truth about me. Unquestionably he was not. Instead his diatribe had *finally* gotten the message through my thick head that there would always be a newspaper ready to swat me if I got close enough to my father for him to reach me emotionally. I knew now that no matter what I did, I was just one more disappointment in his life. He'd be sure to let me know, without fail. It would be emblazoned in bright lights two-feet tall on a theater marquee.

By tearing me down, he seemed to somehow make himself feel better about himself. If I were so awful, he was not so bad by comparison. Besides, off-loading his deficiencies on me, he did not have to feel them poke at his consciousness. He obviously had to keep them out of his awareness. As I later learned, a person can only stand so much self-deprecation without being destroyed by it. So when he could make everyone else be "less," he could feel himself be "more."

As things went on, it was obvious he needed to do that more and more frequently. So I had to keep away from him. I was no longer going to be his in-person victim although I knew I was still, to a degree, his internal victim. My K.H. was feeling she had finally had enough with my non-assertiveness and wanted me to flex my standing up for my rights with him. But I couldn't quite do that. Yet I could still recall Leesport and how great it had felt to stand up to my father about the wounded bird.

When I was younger, if I did something he didn't like or said something he considered inappropriate for his child to say to him, he switched my bare legs with a slender, flexible forsythia branch. It stung exquisitely and left inflamed lash marks. He also used his leather belt on occasion but found the twig more suitable when he could find one. Maybe he liked the threatening swishing sound it made. The snapping of the two leather sides of the belt together didn't communicate the same ominousness. Threat was a necessary component in creating fear to make his idea of punishment effective.

But by this time he no longer relied on physical punishment to make me take notice. Now I was old enough that he could use psychological punishment which cut to the heart even more deeply. It left no obvious physical marks, only emotional scars. He found many ways to use it.

While I was at high school play rehearsal (I was "Dr. Janet" in a mystery-comedy, "Lunatics At Large"), my mother had gone into the heavily treed backyard of our apartment to walk Snoopy, our new Pointer puppy. We resided on the second floor of the owner's house on Main Street. There was also a large one-room apartment out back. As she walked around the yard with Snoopy pulling on her leash, my mother inadvertently stepped on a broken branch. It twisted, leaped up, and jabbed her sharply in the leg, just below the knee. It made a deep gash, revealing the tibia beneath. It bled profusely.

When she called out for help, the owners and their two children were not home. My father was in Sherborn visiting my Uncle Barry for some undetermined period of time. The only people who heard her were the two young men who lived in the backyard apartment. They ran to her rescue. As one made a compression bandage and tourniquet out of dish towels for her leg, the other took Snoopy back upstairs to our apartment and secured my mother's handbag for her.

Then the two drove her immediately into town, with one of them keeping compression on her wound, to the local doctor. He put a large clamp on the wound instead of suturing it. After the young men had her prescription filled at the drug store, they brought her back home. Making sure she was settled in and comfortable with her leg elevated, they gave her some aspirin for pain. Her antibiotic was by her side. They refilled her glass with ice to give her something cool to sip. Then they waited for me to arrive home.

Before they departed, my mother called my father to let him know the situation. They solicitously made sure she was in need of nothing more. They made her promise that if she required *any* further assistance, she would let them know. They left, going down the back stairs to their apartment. Marveling at this kindness, we were so grateful to them and thanked them profusely.

When my father arrived home an hour later, he heard about the incident in detail. He became livid. He shouted at my mother, demanding to know why she hadn't called him to be the one to drive her to the doctor. Somewhere in his harangue was lost the fact that she had been seriously injured and might have died without immediate help. But he was beside himself with anger—not only with her but also with the two young men who had helped her.

He was sure they were homosexuals. "They shouldn't have helped you. They shouldn't have touched you. They shouldn't have had access to the apartment to put Snoopy away much less to get your purse. They shouldn't have put you in their car to take you to the doctor. They shouldn't have stayed with you until she came home." My mother and the seriousness of her accident were ignored in his self-indulgent raving. It was all about him. It was all about his place as master of his realm and controlling all within it.

When my father lost his temper, there was no rationality. He couldn't have realistically expected her to get to a phone on the second floor with a bone-exposing hole in her leg. This was not the era of cell phones. He seemed to have expected her to lie in the yard, bleeding copiously, counting the many minutes until he arrived, whenever that would be. Even if she had somehow reached a phone to call to him before she fainted from shock, apparently she was still supposed to have lain there and waited and waited and waited. My father was raising brutal insensitivity to a virtue and making himself a candidate for sainthood.

Were they gay? Who knew. And who cared! They saved my mother's life. But my father was so entrenched in the possibility of their being homosexual that he couldn't get his antagonisms straight. He certainly couldn't have been concerned for her safety in their company if they were gay. If they were gay, they weren't likely to "sexually molest" her. Oh, puhleeze!

They were acting like good Samaritans, altruistically helping a fellow human being in an emergency. That was something to rejoice about. But like so many others my father negatively evaluated, he presumed they were different—lesser—so he placed them at a lowest link on the medieval Golden Chain between the Supreme Being and the beasts of the field. However, I thought all that was really secondary to his simply having been supremely miffed that they, or *anyone* else, had done what he didn't do, couldn't have done, but felt he should have done—not for her, but for himself.

They deserved to be further lauded and appreciated for their thoughtful, rational, and swift action. But sadly we couldn't invite them to dinner. My father would have spared them no indirect disparagement. His passive-aggressive tactics to show his displeasure were legendary. His bigotry and disregard for others extended well beyond African-Americans, Jews, Hispanics, Catholics, Poles, et al. It all boiled down to the premise that if you weren't my father, J. W. the First, you had no value.

While I didn't feel I could contradict him and face his wrath, my K.H. would have stopped him in his tracks as he blamed everyone for his own perceived deficiencies. She would have re-directed the focus to my mother's condition. "She could have died waiting for you. But she was saved by people who could have been purple with chartreuse antennae for all it mattered. Get your priorities straight."

CHAPTER 23

Piling On More Humiliations

In my freshman year at Millis High School we had a driving course to help us learn what we needed to know to be better and safer drivers. Having a course-completion certificate would also reduce my insurance cost. But my father decided that he should be the one to teach me to drive since he was a "perfect" driver. I begged off. "No, no, that's okay. I'm scheduled for the course at school." But he was not to be dissuaded. When he wanted to do something, he did it, like always snapping my bra in the back at home which I disliked, felt was disrespectful, and asked him repeatedly to stop doing. It made no impression on his behavior. Again, if he wanted to do it, he did it. So that evening he drove us to the empty school parking lot. We changed seats. And everything went downhill from there.

I was extremely nervous with him looking over my shoulder, examining and evaluating every little move I made or didn't make. "Let the clutch out slowly with your left foot as you increase the gas with your right." That sounds easy to do but isn't until you get the coordination down. I popped the clutch, letting it up too quickly so the car hopped forward then stalled. "You stalled the car. Do you know why you did that?"

Impatiently he kept telling me what to do. I kept doing it wrong as if I had no connection whatsoever between my brain, hands, and feet. When I'd shift gears, I did so incompletely, making a loud grinding sound which provoked more accusations and comments from him.

"You're going to ruin the gearing. Make sure the car is in gear before releasing the clutch. No, you're doing it wrong. You have to push through the gate for it to be in gear." Huh? "Push the clutch in all the way, now shift gears. No. You haven't shifted properly. That's not first gear. Careful! You're going to go into reverse. Don't you know the difference between first and reverse?" I hadn't yet developed the touch I needed for this or any standard-shift car. Furthermore, I either gave the car too little gas or too much gas, no matter what I was trying to do, causing it to either stall or race.

My incredibly bad performance convinced him that he did not want to go through this muscle-tightening, mind-numbing, blood-pressure-raising frustration ever again with me. I was a nervous wreck when I arrived home but, at least, I was reasonably sure there wouldn't be a call for a second lesson. By being so uncoordinated, I had persuaded him I was hopeless. There was no question that I had lucked out this time. My K.H. told me, "There's no need to do anything. Let *him* decide it wasn't worth his time." And, in fact, I went on to become an excellent driver with a standard shift in spite of that tranquilizer-demanding trial run.

Over my four years in high school I struggled through a series of embarrassing events which made me look even more like an outsider in three situations and a liar in another. Our freshman class had decided to go to Boston to see "West Side Story." The tickets were $2 at that time so I had bought one with part of my paycheck from working behind the counter at Sunshine Dairy in Millis. I made burgers, fried clams, "frapps," ice cream-thickened milk shakes, and scooped ice cream, when I wasn't in class. I was pleased to be doing something with the class, finally being a part of the group, with all of us having fun together. But the day before the trip I discovered my family had no money for groceries.

Feeling awkward, I lied, telling my class that I had to go to Vermont to visit my grandfather instead and couldn't go to the movie with them. So I wanted to sell my ticket. Good fortune materialized when Kathy who hadn't gotten a ticket in time bought it from me. Therefore, we could scrape by for another day or so. We were incredibly lucky that food costs were low at that time.

During my sophomore year in one of my father's more high-flying moments, he had decided we were going to emigrate to Australia. His unspoken goal seemed to be to rid himself of his past failures and start afresh. Perhaps without his father peering over his shoulder, demanding his presence at a moment's notice, and expecting him to snap-to to carry out his orders he might be able to turn himself around—at least to some degree.

He did intensive library research—this was well before computers and the World Wide Web. He wrote to the Australian government to learn about plans whereby they would financially help emigrants travel to and establish themselves there. He checked on how to secure passports. He investigated moving costs from Boston to Australia by boat although by this time we had very little furniture or other possessions—mostly the clothes on our backs. Going by ship was supposedly cheaper than the four of us flying.

He was a one-man army of ambition. Australia was all he could talk about for weeks and weeks and weeks. As he collected huge piles of information in file folders, it was soon beginning to look as if *this* time this venture would really happen. I felt it was coming close to a time that I should share our plans with my classmates. I was so tired of moving. I did not want to move anywhere, much less to a new country. The charm of koalas, kangaroos, Tasmanian devils, and having winters when we had summers wasn't enough to reverse my desire not to relocate.

Moving would likely mean I wouldn't be graduated with them. This was something about which I felt really bad. I had broken through by being open and friendly and was continuing to make friends both in and out of school, with the continuing help of my K.H. I didn't want to lose them again. I felt like a seedling, struggling to hang on to my tiny section of turf, but constantly being buffeted by the heavy wind gusts trying their best to dislodge me.

Of course, having been a student of my father's history, I should have known better than to have offered a peep about Australia. I should have kept mum until we were packed and physically ensconced on the boat. Because it wasn't long before my father began to lose all his unmitigated enthusiasm about moving. It dwindled little by little, drip by drip, day by day until after nearly six months there was no further discussion of it. The monumental excursion simply faded away like a magnificent multi-colored sunset into the dull grays of twilight. No one brought it up to my father because you couldn't predict how he'd respond.

It was soon obvious to everyone that I wasn't leaving. This left my classmates looking askance at me, commenting snidely, "I thought you were going to Australia," to which I had no satisfactory reply. I'd fallen for my father's extravagant line of wishful thinking again. There was only myself to blame for the consequential humiliation I felt in trying to explain the change in plans without implicating my father. My K.H. said, "Don't bother. They'll think what they want."

In my junior year I headed the Decorating Committee for the Junior Prom which I felt meant I was making real social inroads. I finally saw myself as a part of my class. Full of ideas and enthusiasm, I had visions of helping make this prom particularly artistic and beautiful for everyone. It was at this moment I made my first mistake. I worked on my designs at home. When my father saw and questioned me about what I was doing, I smartly dismissed it. Instead of saying I was on a committee, much less the head of it, I simply mentioned that the class was seeking ideas for a prom theme. But this inadvertently alerted him to the fact the prom was approaching. I had since learned that if I had said anything more, my father would have used this opportunity to continue to impose his "expertise" on what I should do and how I should do it.

The committee decided on one of my designs, a Japanese tea garden, in the new gymnasium. We had been in the new school building with its highly-polished, carefully-constructed gym floor for only two years. For the committee's consideration, I sketched possible design components and arrangements, made suggestions about names, materials needed, and how materials could be secured to walls and floor without nails or other damaging attachments. Everything was moving along agreeably until some members stated that they wanted to add real water to the proposed pond. Up to that point, we had been working with the idea of having a resemblance of water in the camouflaged child's pool that would go under the small Japanese footbridge. It was at this moment that I made my second "mistake."

Gathering up all my assertiveness, I opposed the idea of real water. The principal had already met with me as committee chair to warn me about causing *any* kind of destruction—major or minor—to the floor or walls. I shared the principal's issues with them. My concern was that a child's thin plastic pool was vulnerable to snags and punctures by a sharp edge or point—a wood splinter, staple, thumb tack, nail, or a high heel shoe. If it held water, the likelihood of leakage seemed too great to chance it. As both a committee member and the chair, I felt I had a responsibility to reduce the probabilities of harm, even if it made me a wet blanket.

Despite our ongoing disagreement on that item, the theme and decorations progressed for several weeks with the prom name, scrolls with Japanese symbols, cherry tree in blossom, and preliminary construction of the front of the tea house with its railing, "glass" door, and roof, and the wooden footbridge. Then things changed dramatically.

All the other committee members had coalesced around the idea of having water in the pool. They stated they thought I was being picky, dogmatic, and unnecessarily obstructive in opposing it. As a result, they wanted someone with whom they could work in more harmonious agreement. Asking Roger, a senior who had headed the prom decorating committee the year before, to be their new chair, they unceremoniously ousted me as soon as he said "yes." I didn't know if they had the power to dump me, but it seemed futile to fight my expulsion since we'd have to work "together" to finish the project on time. Unlike me, Roger wasn't worried about having a water leak or any other problem. In fact, he was as jubilant as they were about having real water. He thrust himself into his new role with gusto.

For me this was suddenly my first day at high school all over again. I was an outcast, once again seemingly "unacceptable." My K.H. told me, "Just ignore it. Their enthusiasm is outweighing their reasoning. Your concerns are rational and responsible. They want someone who shares their enthusiasm and Roger is nothing if not enthusiastic. If the pool doesn't leak, everyone will enjoy the prom irrespective of who headed the committee. If it leaks, he'll be 'responsible' but in name only. In reality, no one but 'management' will give a damn."

Disappointed and depressed by their rejection of me, I quickly decided I would not attend the dance. With several weeks to go before the event I still had no date. No one had asked me. In my heart of hearts, I didn't expect anyone to do so. While I got along with

128

everyone in general, I wasn't really close to any males in school. When I infrequently dated, it was with those outside Millis High School, former graduates or men in college. Dejectedly I wondered if maybe things hadn't changed that much after all since my time as a freshman.

Years later I associated this situation with when Janice Joplin returned to her oil refinery hometown of Port Arthur, Texas, in 1970 for her tenth high school reunion. Despite her having been a conservative teen like her high school classmates, she had been emotionally-scarred in high school. She had been laughed at by classmates and called "pig," due to her increasing weight and facial acne. (Fortunately that was not my problem.)Upon her reunion arrival, a local reporter insensitively asked her why she hadn't attended her own high school prom. Her heartbreakingly revealing straight answer was, "No one asked me." This mirrored her reception at the University of Texas shortly thereafter where she was nominated as "The Ugliest Man on Campus." She left her reunion as she had left high school and U.T.: feeling unloved and rejected. Maybe pre-hippie Janice Joplin and I had something in common.

Immediately I began justifying my snap-decision not to attend. I told myself it would save me spending money to buy a dress I would likely never wear again. I wouldn't be comfortable going alone where everyone else had a date. I'd feel humiliated as everyone raved about Roger's decorations, knowing I'd been tossed out on my ear for standing up against risking something as "dumb" as a water leak. I knew I was never going to be "Miss Popularity" at M.H.S. but being a contrary voice about decorations had made me an obvious outsider all over again.

Okay, I asked myself, what *really* was the big deal about not going? I hadn't been to *other* class functions; but, of course, that was for a very different reason. Besides, no one was going to miss me if I didn't go. They'd be involved in their own individual situations, with friends, dancing, and having fun. My emotional justification made me feel better but only for a few minutes. There was a much larger—very real problem—with my not attending the prom.

That problem was my father. I had kept my mouth shut about my rejection because there was no need to give him more ammunition against me. But, irrespective, he knew the prom was approaching. After all, I was submitting designs for it. He'd expect me to go because that was what I should do as a junior. In an instant I knew it wasn't as clear cut as I'd thought it would be. What was I going to do about my not going in that circumstance? I couldn't even hint at my not having been invited. That would have relegated me to being treated like "super-flop" again. And then he'd never let me forget—by word or gesture—that he had been "right" all along when he excoriated me three years earlier for being a personal and social failure.

Furthermore, I couldn't see how I could fake my going with nothing appropriate to wear and no one to pick me up. My tortured soul was crying out, but my K.H. was already whispering, "You need to stand back to get some perspective on it before you make any hard and fast decisions. Check out your realistic options. Stow the emotion. It's only getting in your way. You *can* work this out. We can work this out together." I thought, yeah, sure.

Mr. Vellardo, the principal, was someone with whom I had spoken on numerous occasions about my parents' constant fighting that had me tied in stressful knots. He was kind and a good listener. As a result, I provided his office with Big Band 45-rpm records to be played over the public address system in the cafeteria during lunch. It should have been no surprise to me that after I had mentioned in passing my committee rejection and my not attending the prom, my classmate, Ron, the son of Mr. Vellardo's secretary, asked me to be his prom date. Now what would I do? Emotionally I didn't want to go, but rationally I had to go.

His asking felt like the scenario out of a silent film about the rescue of the "poor little flower girl, dressed in rags, selling her artificial wares in the snow." I was so conflicted. I needed to avoid my father's guaranteed harassment over my "not having been invited." It would have been hard to avoid and unbearable. But I still was hanging on to my humiliation about my rejection. Initially, I had thanked Ron but said I was going to Vermont instead. Perhaps sensing that what I said was a lie to try to save face, he spoke to me after school, reassuring me, "I would have asked you early on but I thought you would already have a date." My mind was swirling.

My K.H. was now shouting in my ear, "Get your priorities straight! There is nothing to be humiliated about. There was a disagreement. You did what you thought was right. Remember what Eleanor Roosevelt said: 'Do what you feel in your heart to be right for you'll be criticized anyway. You'll be damned if you do, and damned if you don't.' Big damn deal! So get over it—and then go with Ron! You're letting self-pitying emotions rule your actions! That can only cause more problems for you. Become smart. You have only ONE *real* problem. You can solve it by going with Ron."

I asked him if I could give him my answer the next day, which would still give him plenty of time to then ask someone else. In my feeling sorry for myself I interpreted what he said to me to be a very kind, thoughtful excuse for asking me late but my K.H. was right. I was letting my ego get in the way. I was being irrational. On the one hand, I didn't want to be asked *just* because people "felt sorry" for me. My K.H. said, "Who gives a rat's butt *why* you were asked? You shouldn't! He asked you. That's what's important!" But, on the other, going with Ron would pragmatically solve my looming problem with my father. It seemed like such an easy decision to make, but I was still wavering.

The next morning early, before my first class, Mr. Vellardo called me into his office. With a serious expression on his craggy face he said, "You have a choice to make." Then he laid down the law, "I want you to go to the prom. The business about the decoration committee while painful is incidental. It's not as important as your being a member of this class. This is *your* prom, irrespective of anything else.

"Yes, you had a good reason to fight against having water in the pond; you knew I am vehemently opposed to anything that could potentially damage the floor. You stood your ground on your principles against the committee. That was a very hard thing to do and you did it. Congratulations.

"However, that has *nothing* to do with *your* attendance at *your* prom. *If* you don't go with Ron who I know has asked you, Mrs. Vellardo and I *will* escort you. But I don't think you'd like that because that could be pretty embarrassing all around. Go with Ron. I am *not* asking you; I am telling you. Do you understand me?" I nodded again, intimidated, conflicted, wanting to cry.

Of course, I couldn't let the principal and his wife escort me to the prom which I'm sure they would actually do. That wouldn't be just embarrassing; that would be weird and pathetic. Everyone would mutter, "Oh my God! She couldn't even get a date and *had* to have the principal drag her here. How pitiful is that? I'd rather die than let the principal, and his wife, bring me to the prom. Damn! It just goes to show you what a loser she really is and always has been!" And I couldn't even contemplate what my father would say.

My K.H. shouted at the top of her lungs, "LISTEN TO ME, NOW! To hell with the stupid decorations committee rejection, what others might say, and with your being embarrassed by your circumstance. It's all emotional horse manure. Ron is your solution to your father's finding out about the prom and emotionally stretching you on his rack.

"You like Ron. He's a very nice person, good-looking, and you've always gotten along with him. So what's the problem? You have an offer that can save you. You can *choose* to take it and have a fun time with him as well ... or not choose it and suffer at the hands of your father again. Quit your lollygagging. CHOOSE it!"

Resigned, I knew my K.H. was right. I was allowing myself to be hypnotized by my vampire and sink into quicksand again. It was then I also realized what a good friend Mr. Vellardo was being to me by kicking my butt in the right direction. He was acting like the father I never had or ever imagined. When I told Ron I'd go, he seemed genuinely pleased. Now I acknowledged I'd been rescued—not only by Ron but also by my K.H. and Mr. Vellardo. I was feeling very fortunate indeed to have them on my team.

Immediately my mother and I went shopping for something prom-like. I found a sleeveless, scoop-necked, fitted pink lace-bodice cocktail dress with a drop-waist organza full skirt—something I could conceivably wear another time as well. Wearing drop pearl earrings and no other jewelry, a long white chiffon scarf draped across my throat hanging down the back, with my blonde hair in a long pageboy, and with white satin high heels, I was all set. Pinning on the gardenia shoulder corsage Ron bought for me, I arrived proudly at the prom with him. Ron, likewise, was all decked out in his black-tuxedo finest, smiling, looking very handsome.

Doing as my K.H. had commanded, I had deep-sixed my decorations' humiliation even though a small part of me anticipated and was primed for the worst. But, delightfully, no one said a word to me about the decorations' debacle. Everyone was having too good a time to care about such trivia, assuming they had heard the gossip. It was obvious I had blown the situation w-a-y out of proportion.

In spite of the fact the gym decorations seemed to me to be grotesquely overdone, looking more like a garish carnival midway than a serene and simple Japanese tea garden, I let myself be captured by the celebratory atmosphere all around me. Everyone was in high spirits. Ron was funny and fun; and I truly enjoyed myself. Everything else became unimportant.

However, toward the end of the evening before we left for dinner, I discovered something that caused me to shake my head and snicker to myself. Ahh. It was silent vindication. The water feature had been punctured by some unknown object and had leaked all over that end of the gym's floor. Soaking for hours, the water caused the wood to swell, requiring expensive repairs. And my K.H. was right again. No one really cared, except Mr. Vellardo. And it was only he who would have to reap the repercussions.

I did finish high school in Millis but not before I had to bow out of the senior class trip to Washington, D.C. I had desperately wanted to share it with my now four-years' worth of friends. But this time I kept my mouth shut. I showed enthusiasm for everyone else's plans. I was weary of making excuses for the things that went on in my private life over which I felt I had no control. My K.H. said, "Don't bother lying about why you're not going. It's nobody's business. Just change the subject back onto them about their plans when you're asked. Then wish them to have a great time" Even with my working full-time, there was no way I could financially swing it. So once again, that was that.

CHAPTER 24

Abandoning My Pets Again

Though it didn't seem possible that things could get any worse, they continued to slide down the slippery slope. We lost the car my father used. We were repeatedly asked to move when we couldn't pay the rent. It was a broken record. When we found ourselves at a particularly low ebb of our financial situation, we were down to our very last fifty cents. Cliché-like, we actually gathered it from scavenging under the sofa cushions.

In spite of the reality of our not even having a loaf of bread in the house to eat, my father stated he needed to buy a pack of cigarettes for himself. Again I argued inadequately with my father about it. *His* addiction—*his* thoughts, *his* feelings, and *his* actions—always came first. Never acknowledging his physical dependence, he'd feed his need for nicotine before he would feed his family. Hate for him continued to percolate inside me, burning my insides.

His behaviors became more peculiar. After moving from Main Street to Dover Road in Millis, he decided to take out the railing for the stairs going to the second floor in the rental house. He stated with impetuosity he was going to replace it. "This railing is unsafe. It has a jiggle. It really should be replaced. I'll put in a new one" The problem was twofold. One, he never approached a job with care and deliberation. He never considered what his options might be. He never carefully selected the best-fit option and then made a plan accordingly. Two, he never considered that this wasn't his house to repair or deconstruct as he chose. If the railing had a problem, he should have contacted the owner to have someone fix it properly.

Uncomprehending his proposal, I tried to argue with him. I knew that it would fall on deaf ears. His response was his usual, "I will if I want to." I could never grasp why he thought he had to totally replace it. The movement was very slight. It seemed to me it could have used a little bit of bracing, perhaps with L-brackets, or re-seating, re-cementing of the newel post. It functioned satisfactorily otherwise. It wasn't really unsafe from my perspective. But rationality had nothing to do with his desire to remove it. My mother tried but couldn't talk him out of it. It was a fool's errand because he never listened to her anyway. He had never listened to anyone but his father. So with saw in hand, he happily separated the balustrade from the stair treads, leaving a large open space which now was, in reality, unsafe.

Then after the railing disappeared, a month clicked by and nothing had taken its place. Ascending and descending the stairs became tricky, especially if you had anything in your arms, like laundry, or if you couldn't comfortably hug your back or your side to the wall. All his effusiveness for reconstruction seemed to evaporate from him. It was as if dry air had drawn all his hot sweat of eagerness away, leaving him cooler and less interested. In essence, he no longer observed the situation as a problem to solve. He had cured the railing of its unreliability.

Beyond my trying to persuade my father otherwise, my K.H. would have argued harder about no need to remove the railing. She would have demanded he listen, made suggestions about what could be done instead. If necessary, she would have hammered some 30-penny nails into it for good measure. If that didn't work, she would have been on his case until he put something "safe" in its place, assuming he had any idea what he was doing.

Before we left Millis, Snoopy, who was, surprisingly, still with us ran into Dover Road. She was struck by a car, smashing her left back leg. Because my father said he felt his animals should run free, he had allowed her to gallivant wherever she pleased. This was despite the concerns of my mother and me about the potential danger from cars and other animals. He apparently hadn't learned that lesson in Leesport with Stuffy and Spooky. Or perhaps, more likely, he didn't want to walk her as I had been doing when I was home.

The extent of her injuries required a large cast that looked like a small ironing board and a large outlay of cash. Where that came from I didn't know. She frequently tried to climb the railing-less stairs to get to my room. Trying to ascend with or without the railing, she was putting herself in grave jeopardy. Poor gentle Snoopy often shivered with anxiety. As a result of my father's frequent rages, she seemed to feel insecure about what the anger meant. It often filtered down to her in negative nonverbal behaviors. Calm when my father purchased her, she became hyper and very needy.

Because of her wanting to be with me, irrespective of the cast she was dragging around behind her, I began sleeping on the sofa in the living room. In front of the stone fireplace she could be with me in relative safety after I moved the other furniture on which she could snag her cast. Trying to comfort and pet her, I managed very little sleep. She wanted so badly to crawl onto the sofa to snuggle with me, her protector. Despite her unwieldy appendage making it impossible, she kept trying. That her leg would repair itself correctly seemed unlikely. She too was a victim in more ways than one.

Later, when we had to move again, this time Snoopy and Sam could not follow. As a result, I spent one whole Saturday driving around the countryside with them looking for a place where they could be adopted. The bones in Snoopy's leg had healed but the leg muscles around it had atrophied. Unsuccessfully I had tried to provide her with effective doggie physical therapy. Hanging uselessly, her limb still seemed to provide her with more balance, perhaps, than if her leg had been amputated. But maybe that was just my wishful thinking.

Late in the day I discovered a property west of Marlborough. It was twelve miles away from Millis, in the country with fields and trees and on a quiet street. Playing happily in the front yard were a cat and dog. As I opened the car door, the dog rushed toward me, tongue lolling, showing its cheerfulness in seeing me. The cat sauntered over too, curling its tail around my leg in greeting. Speaking with the animals' human companions, I tried to explain the situation without breaking down.

"We have to move and can't take Snoopy and Sam with us. She's a sweet gentle dog who'll be a good companion. She loves to run and her back leg doesn't get in her way. Sam's a cuddly baby who gets along with everyone. Would you consider adopting them, giving them the loving home they need? I can't provide it to them any longer." My voice cracked more than once.

The man and woman seemed sincere when they said, "We'll be happy to take Snoopy and Sam. It doesn't matter about her leg. I'm sure she'll fit in well with Mike and Frisky. There's lots of room for her to run around and have fun. Frisky likes other cats." I could only hope that was true.

Forlornly I trudged back to the car to let them out. I picked up Sam and cuddled him in my arms and Snoopy hopped along beside me. I took them to meet their new parents. I put Sam down and Frisky sniffed him with no hissing. Mike playfully threw a paw onto Snoopy's shoulders, jumped up and down, and trotted away, looking back. Snoopy immediately followed. Despite Frisky and Mike likewise seeming to welcome them, I felt I was abandoning my babies.

The people seemed kind. Their animals seemed well-nourished and happy. Snoopy could run all she wanted and now would have a companion with which to run and play. Sam now had a companion too with which to mock fight, cuddle, and sleep. But how could I leave them? I closed my fist tightly on my car keys, my knuckles turning white, until I risked drawing blood. I had to remind myself they were going into an environment that had potential for being so much more comfortable and comforting than where they had been. Tears still dropped down my cheeks onto the steering wheel as I departed Marlborough. I thought I shouldn't have to do this. My K.H. lauded me for doing the right thing despite the accompanying, lingering pain, guilt, and anger.

CHAPTER 25

Leaving But Never Escaping

After high school, I went to Baylor University in Waco, Texas, because of their pre-med program and their top-ranked medical school in Houston, just three hours away. Being away from home was a two-sided coin. On one side, I was so glad to be away from my family's storms and stress. But on the other, I worried incessantly about what was going on, about my father's physical health and behavior and my mother's emotional health.

To arrive home for Christmas from Baylor I had negotiated heavy snow storms from Texas to Massachusetts, in a dorm mate's VW Beetle in a two-day driving marathon. I arrived late in the evening. As I walked in, and before I could shake the snow off my boots, my brother insulted my mother, "How can you be so STUPID!" he mimicked my father. He was always trying to keep on my father's good side.

In my exhaustion my submerged anger immediately leaped to the surface with a vengeance. Blood vessels in my neck bulging, my face nearly purple, I shouted at my brother, "Don't you DARE talk to your mother like that!"

Without a nanosecond of hesitation, my father jumped into the impending fisticuffs, "Mind your own business!" he sharply commanded me, never uttering a rebuke to my brother. I felt the blow as if physically assaulted. I couldn't decide whether to cry, riddle him with F-words which surely would have gotten his attention and me a real slap in the mouth, or kill him. In my state of lowered tolerance the latter was very appealing and only a muscle twitch away. My K.H. would not have done anything, however, because the situation was too volatile. But I would have liked her to have given both my father and brother a couple of roundhouse punches to get their attention and then have told them, with a steely stare, to "cut the crap or else."

I could only imagine the constant barrage my mother had suffered at the hands of this strange father-son alliance in my absence. Each egged on, fed off, and reinforced the other one in this malevolent *folie à deux*. But in my bottomless anger, disappointment, and disillusionment, I had to keep physicality out of the interaction. All I could do was clench my jaw tight and utter a lame, "I wish I'd never come home. Everything is still the same."

My father, his face contorted in rage, started to say, "Well, you can just lea ...," then stopped cold—his declaration hanging in air. Even angry, he knew he couldn't go too far. No matter how many "I will if I want to's" he had responded over the years, this was not a situation in which to speak so cavalierly. He needed me and he knew it. He couldn't let me abandon him. After I had been away for four months, I had unrealistically hoped that for this one holiday with all of us together things could conceivable have changed for the better, even a miniscule amount.

For my mother's sake, I kept my fury under control. My father kept his criticism of her to a minimum in my presence, perhaps worried I might actually commit assault and battery, if not homicide. He was wise to do that. One evening when she was ironing some shirts in the kitchen, my mother whispered to me, "You don't want to do this." It was rife with many meanings but I took it as an explicit and implicit warning to be aware and carefully consider my options so I would not end up like her.

It had occurred to me that physically attacking my father wouldn't change anything positively for her. In fact, it would likely have done just the opposite. He would then have projected his anger with me onto her. My brother fortunately disappeared for the rest of my visit except for Christmas Day. For the day he was smart enough to keep his vitriol to himself. I hated his guts.

After that, back at school, I knew I could no longer stay at Baylor, despite its path to physician-hood. I had tied myself into half-hitches and granny knots over the situation at home. As a result of my internal turmoil, my skin began to show it. My face and neck were

139

now covered with itching, oozing red scabs. One Waco doctor labeled it as "neurodermatitis." He prescribed a cream which had some kind of grit in it. It burned. It made my condition worse. He said it couldn't and didn't.

In my low ebb I emulated my K.H. and argued with him about continuing on his treatment regimen. I refused to adhere to his instructions, "I understand what you're saying but I'm not using this stuff irrespective of what you say about it," and discontinued the medication.

He said, "You're being stupid. You're not the doctor. I am! I know what will make you better. You have no idea. You only think the medication is making your skin condition worse. You're either not applying it right or haven't been using it long enough. You must be doing something wrong if it burns and doesn't seem to be working. You're imagining that it has grit in it because it isn't made that way. It doesn't make you very smart to quit your treatment. If you choose not to comply with my instructions, don't bother coming back. I won't treat someone who won't do as I say."

Wholeheartedly agreeing, my K.H. cheered me on. I reared my assertiveness and I told him, "No, I totally disagree. It's not my fault. I am using this cream as prescribed and it's not working. I know my own body and how it is responding. This medication has grit in it. It burns and isn't helping me. You're right. You will not see me again because I have no intention of continuing to follow your instructions." That felt so liberating!

Working after class and nights at my dormitory switchboard, I made a little money that helped defray some of my living costs. There was no money coming from home. But each night I lay in bed, staring at the ceiling, feeling I should be home helping my mother. At the same time, I was trying not to let my pillowcase stick to my un-bandaged super-wet lesions. The sores had begun to spread. Starting with my face and throat, they were now on my chest and breasts as well. The itching and discomfort were indescribable. All fabric adhered to my seeping sores. This included my cotton bras, short nightgowns, bed sheets, or gauze bandages. When the fabrics shifted, scabs were torn from the wounds, creating even more seepage, itching, and pain. This didn't leave me with any other choices.

Furthermore, I was looking more leprous by the day. The next morning following my sleepless night, I would be exhausted. Invariably I fell asleep in 7 a.m. classes. This led to my being upbraided each time by a professor's inappropriately sarcastic reprimand.

When I was caught asleep, there is nothing I could say to pretend I wasn't. When I tried to make it work the second time around, I responded to whatever the instructor seemed to be saying as I awoke. But I was saying "gribblezook" to his question about "farfel-farfel pippick." That was the last time I bothered to try. After that, it happened so often that I just let them feel insulted that I wasn't supremely stimulated by their lectures and then feel avenged by their childishly mouthing off at me.

The following summer, I left Baylor to return to Massachusetts, thin, haggard, but with my sores well on their way to healing—without that medication. My mother and father were only sporadically making ends meet. With my strong support, my mother declared she was going to find a job. She had wanted to do this for many years but my father had vehemently opposed it. She had been afraid to contradict him.

When she stated her intent, my father was beside himself with rage, shouting dictatorially, "No wife of mine is going to work!" Of course, what he meant was "no wife of mine is going to get a job" because she had worked very hard for nearly twenty years trying to keep their sad lives rolling along, however shakily. It was she who had kept them on as even a keel as was possible under the direst of circumstances. Strangely, my father seemed to think it was more reasonable or honorable to starve to death than to let my mother bring in the money they needed. My K.H. yelled, "Bravo!"

Shortly thereafter, to my amazement my father gave me a second-hand, 1957 turquoise and white Chevy convertible with white interior and standard shift. I cleaned and polished until I was sure I'd wear off the paint. I don't know how he managed it, which concerned me a lot. But I was thrilled to have my own car. I drove it only twice with the top down, my waist-length hair flying in a ponytail behind me, all around Millis as soon as I received it. All I needed was a long, white silk scarf to drape around my neck, aviator sunglasses, and leather driving gloves. I would be such "hot stuff."

However, my looking like a freedom-loving celebrity lasted only those two days. That is until I realized that for my mother to work she needed my car for transportation. After she and I both secured jobs, the arrangement quickly became that she would drop me off at one of my jobs before going to hers. And in between I would borrow rides from friends or colleagues or take the bus to get to the other one. At night I would walk to the theater to drive home with her. That immediately deflated my special gift balloon.

CHAPTER 26

Deciding Whose Pain is Justified

Without much hunting, she had found a sales job at an exclusive dress shop at Shopper' World Mall in Natick, on the lower level. There she would model the dresses for customers when necessary. She also had become a ticket taker at the mall's theater at night, on the upper level. I had taken a Saturday and nights part-time managerial job at The Book Nook, a record and book store there on the lower level of that mall below the theater. I also became a counter worker at a restaurant in the Kreskin Mall down Route 9 to the east.

I continued these while I went to school at Framingham State College. They provided me with the one hundred dollars per semester funding at FSC as well as help for my family financially. There was no way I wasn't going back to my education even though I had been sidelined from medicine for a while. Besides, these two jobs and school had another benefit. They helped keep me away from my father as much as possible.

However, the two jobs plus school added to my stress and fatigue. At the restaurant, I saw hamburgers being dropped on the greasy, filthy, sawdust-covered floor in the kitchen and replaced on the grill. The owner and executive staff of Kreskin came in for lunch and expected special privileges about which no one told me. No one had even pointed out the people of whom I was supposed to be aware so I could "genuflect" before them.

I spent a lot of time making spoiling food look palatable again, using mayonnaise that had a thick, gelatinous surface off which I could bounce a quarter. Another time I planned to wash the interior of the milk machine and was told by a restaurant co-manager, not to.

He said, "It'll give customers diarrhea." I didn't understand that. I wasn't going to leave soap in it. It had to be washed, didn't it?

On more than one occasion I was pinned to the wall with accusations of over-charging when the discount-house president ordered a second Kosher dill or something else and I unknowingly charged him five cents for it. "Ewe charge me fur dat secon peekle. I doan gut charge fur dat! Whassa matteh wid you? Doan ewe know who I yam? Doan ewe know ennyting?" Or, he wanted more milk, toast, or more meat on his sandwich, "I won mur muck."

"I'm sorry, what would you like"

"Muck, muck, muck. Ken ewe heah?"

"Oh, milk, I'm sorry. I'll get that for you."

"Bud doan charge me fur id dis time. I doan gut charge fur id. Ewe unnerstan?"

Then one afternoon, after I had been there about four months, I was leaping around like a kangaroo on a pogo stick trying to handle four things at once during peak lunch hour. The raised, slatted platform on the floor behind the counter was always slippery from spills, like greasy chicken soup, mayonnaise, melted butter, cream, sliced tomato or onion. Running from customer to customer, I slipped, sliding three feet along the rails, crashing into the glass case at the front end. I spilled boiling coffee from the cup in my hand all over my shirt front and my neck, barely missing my face.

That was it. I had had it. I raised the coffee cup and saucer high above my head then dashed them with all my strength into a gazillion clay pieces on the floor. Unknowingly, I ran back to the kitchen into the unwelcoming arms of the only person who was there, the Rastafarian-lookalike cook. I was heaving sobs. I felt I was going crazy. I didn't know where I was. I didn't care. My brain was detached from my body. Everything poured out of me. I wailed for ten minutes. My neck and chest burned. I needed ice to stop the burn. I was beyond doing anything about it.

The expression on his face was one of shock and disbelief. What was he supposed to do? His arms uncomfortably half-encircled me, not touching me. Startled, looking around for help, he found there was none forthcoming. Now what could he do? After my ten minutes, I finally unburied my face from his meat-stained, greasy apron. Tears still running down my face further smeared my mascara. I looked like a masked robber. Dazed, I stepped back from my non-rescuer.

Removing myself from his reluctant loose grip, I made my way slowly to where I had left my handbag. Still looking nonplussed, the cook quickly returned to his sputtering hamburgers, which were more like charcoal briquettes at this point, and his grease-spitting pastrami. As if in a dream, I removed my apron, gathered my purse, and mumbled something like, "I quit. You can mail me my check." I had no idea if anyone heard me much less if my words were even intelligible. I didn't care. And my K.H. cheered.

A sandy-haired regular customer who was around my age saw what had occurred. He looked distraught but unsure what to do. As I made my way haltingly toward the front glass door, he rose from his lunch table to escort me out. Even though my tears had ceased, I was shaking all over and my feet hardly seemed to be touching the ground. Outside, I looked around as if desperately searching for my car. He touched my arm and asked, "Is your car here?" I shook my head "no" but continued to distractedly look. Traffic was heavy on Route 9 as well as in the parking lot. Cars were cruising looking for spaces, and pulling in and out. "Can I give you a ride some place? You don't seem to be in any shape to drive." I nodded, mumbling "Shopper's World."

I accepted the ride to wait for my mother there. After about an hour when I had managed to compose myself, I spoke with Mr. Allen, the owner of The Book Nook. I persuaded him to give me more hours, which he did so I could make up for my discarded restaurant job. Even though my K.H. would have left the restaurant sooner than I did, stating, "I'm not going to allow anyone to treat me so badly. I quit!" she still congratulated me for no longer letting them stomp all over me.

To my considerable surprise my father gave me a series of expensive painting lessons with a local artist, Zack Brauen, for my birthday. It was a very thoughtful and insightful present because I was always painting and sketching, especially doing portraiture and abstracts. One of my deep desires was to pursue art in some way, at least as a hobby. People lauded the way my portrait figures' eyes always caught them, connected and communicated with them.

One portrait of my mother was hung in the bank at Shopper's World and the owner of Ken's Steak House contacted me about buying a still life for his restaurant. I truly appreciated the gift from my father but had no idea how he was paying for it. On the one hand, it wasn't appropriate for me to ask how he had purchased it for me. But on the other, I wanted to know from where the money was coming. Specifically, was he using the grocery or bill-paying fund?

But then I showed that appreciation in the most unthinkably insulting way I could for which my father understandably would never forgive me. And I didn't blame him.

In the artist's art shop at Shoppers' World, next to The Book Nook, Brauen had paintings of all genres on consignment. One was a sixty-inch-wide oil painting done in shades of gray, black, and white of New York City's Times Square in the rain. It really caught the ambiance. My mother adored it. After what she had suffered, I wanted to do something really special for her for Christmas. What I did would help tar me as the ultimate traitor in my father's eyes.

After a couple of painting lessons wherein I did a thirty-six by twenty-four still life in oil of a tarnished copper kettle, an aged straw-covered Chianti bottle, and apples, oranges, and grapes on a white linen tablecloth, I asked Zack if I could exchange the remaining lessons for that painting. That plus a few extra bucks made the painting mine. That Christmas eve in our new rental house on Pleasant Street in South Natick I wrapped her painting, stowing it under the sofa. In the meantime my father was dealing with a tippy seven-foot Christmas tree. In his typical frustration, he impulsively nailed it to the living room's hardwood floor with twelve forty-penny, five-inch-long nails.

The next morning I pulled out my mother's special gift and presented it to her. She was so overwhelmed she started to cry. But the look on my father's face almost made me cry too: the sad questioning of how I could have paid for such an important gift. Already knowing full well what I must have done, he asked me anyway.

Feeling both proud and rotten for what I'd done, I told him. I have often wondered if that was a passive-aggressive, in-your-face way of my finally getting back at him. He never said a word. I had pricked his balloon with a sharp pin and he lay crumpled in pieces on the floor. I knew what I had done was cruel. But, at the same time, it was so unlike me to do such a hurtful thing no matter what he had done to me. I had discounted and dismissed his thoughtful gift and the warm emotion behind it. Furthermore, I had turned it into something for my mother, the person my father had claimed was primarily responsible for ruining his life. I had in one fell swoop consigned him and his gift to a lesser consideration of their value.

I regretted doing it. Although I still feel conflicted about it, I cannot say I would not do it again under the same circumstances. My mother truly needed a reminder she was deserving of such a gift. Still, I wish now I could have found another, hopefully kinder, way to have accomplished it. My K.H. acknowledged it, saying, "It was a gutsy thing for you to do. In some situations you have to 'damn the torpedoes, full speed ahead.'"

My father had had a long-time fixation about Christmas presents. It was his rule that everyone had to receive the same *number* of gifts so each of us had to keep track of what we had bought or made. It didn't matter that someone might want one particular thing only. I had to fill in the gaps with meaningless things. It also meant I couldn't target my money for that person's desired gift if there wouldn't be enough money to do that *and* still fill in the other gift slots.

I considered this incomprehensible: Everything had to work out right quantitatively? I constantly worried about what I had gotten for everyone, if they balanced across people, if there were something else that had more meaning I could substitute for some useless plastic knickknack. How could I get them what they said they wanted? It made preparing for Christmas very stressful and took away any of its potential fun.

CHAPTER 27

Not Doing the Right Thing

One Saturday afternoon at The Book Nook, just after the holidays, a nice-looking man came in, looked around at the thirty-three and a third jazz albums, specifically looking for John Coltrane, then approached me to strike up a conversation. It all seemed quite friendly until he asked me, "Would you take off your glasses?" Huh? I thought it odd and debated with myself about his motives. Since I couldn't see without them, it would leave me feeling vulnerable.

"Why?" I asked.

"Because I want to see your eyes," he said. But then, I thought, let's see what this is all about. I thought my eyes were my best feature so maybe he wanted to compliment me on them. Cautiously I acquiesced. However, he practically knocked me flat on the floor with his resulting off-the-wall comment, "You wear too much eye makeup. You're not in New York, you know."

To say I was insulted and angry at his presumptuousness didn't cover it. What a colossal nerve! I thought. Who did he think he was to speak to me like that? Who made him fashion arbiter! Besides, nobody had kicked on his kennel for his opinion. But to my unforgettable shame and regret I never said this to him. In fact, I never opened my mouth in rebuttal. I took the newspaper swat like a puppy that had just wet the floor.

What he said could not stand, but I let it. I stood there, a mass of jelly, with my stomach juices churning. My K.H. would have told this clown, "No one gives a rat's butt for your opinion so shove off, you arrogant turkey!" I was still in shock and trussed up in extreme anger with myself as he casually departed, having blithely put me in "my place" without so much as a whimper from me.

When I arrived home at South Natick, I was still incensed by the interaction. I wanted to dissipate my negative emotion which was like a rat gnawing at my innards. Once again I was "too soon old and too late smart." I fell back on my old, bad habit: I needed to share it. But with whom did I share it? I shared it with my father! But, *this time* I was so absolutely, positively sure he would defend my honor against this obviously cretinous person that I was willing to bet money on it.

I would have lost big time. To my utter, knock-me-down-with-a-feather astonishment, he just looked at me as if amazed I hadn't as yet tumbled to the truth of the man's statement. He pontificated, "He's right, you know." What the ...?! I was struck dumb ... and, maybe, *finally*, had achieved that last little bit of smarts I needed to act in my own behalf, at least as far as he was concerned.

Once again, I couldn't fathom that I had heard him correctly. He was siding with a total stranger against me? And siding with an insulting jerk at that? What was going on here? I cast a glance in the mirror at my "shockingly New York" eye makeup. But all I found was a thin line of brown eyeliner, some brown mascara, and a little Maybelline blonde eyebrow pencil. No fluorescent eye shadow, no false eyelashes. In fact, no heavy makeup, rouged cheeks, or garish lipstick. It was hardly comparable to what someone dancing or acting in a Broadway show or someone stylish shopping on Fifth Avenue would wear.

I shook my head at my incredible stupidity. Would I never learn to just keep my big mouth shut? My K.H. would have dealt with it in the store swiftly and firmly and dismissed it from her mind. She would most assuredly not have given my father the opportunity to demean her.

There was no circumstance on earth in my lifetime that my father was *ever* going to stand up for me, defend me, or come to my rescue. Why? The "boy instead" thing? I didn't really know—and maybe it really *didn't* matter.

My mother's mother, Margretta, had suffered at the hands of my father too. Out of desperation, she had come to stay with us in a back bedroom in our house in South Natick. He didn't want her there and complained bitterly about it. At every opportunity he would disparage her within range of her hearing. "How long is that old bag going to stay? She's so nasty to me and she's in the way." But, he still had the chutzpah to impose on her, to ask to "borrow" a hundred dollars from her. She barely could afford it but gave it to him all the same. He never repaid it. I suspect he felt he deserved it because of her negative feelings about him, feelings which he felt he didn't deserve.

When my mother contracted a severe case of pneumonia, it was my grandmother who tended to her twenty-four/seven, giving my mother her medication, applying hot compresses to her chest, feeding her by hand and keeping her fluids up—actually being the one who saved her life. Still my father couldn't stop his criticism of her. "Is she going to cook that Norwegian crap, fish balls, again? Kee-rist! When is she going to cook us some real American food." My grandmother had long despised him for how he had treated my mother. She came to stay with us for a short time only out of absolute necessity.

My K.H. would have set my father straight at the outset, stating, "She has helped us when we needed it and now were returning the kindness to her. You don't have to like it. But you do have to make the best of it while it lasts ... which means keeping your mouth shut unless you can say something pleasant. And, don't ask her for money."

My grandmother held back her anger and comments only because she needed to after her husband had died of an embolism that had migrated to his lung following prostate surgery. She had no one but my mother left. My mother's father was the sweetest man. He was a Norwegian ship's captain with master's papers. During World War II when the Germans invaded Norway, he moved his family to the U.S., to Clifton, New Jersey. Unfortunately, the only work he could find was on an assembly line, which was well beneath his education, skills, and experience level. He was short, slim, balding, and gentle. He had a smile that lit you with a warm glow. He so loved and missed the sea.

I used to kid him about where he would part the few strands of hair he had on the top of his head. He would just smile and hug me. He knew I was crazy about him. He loved gardening, had flowers, tomatoes, and squash, a small black and white dog, named Spotty, and a box turtle he named Patsy. She lived among his rose of Sharon bushes. He would feed, pet, and talk to her regularly as he let Spotty run happily around the yard of their first-floor apartment. They were inseparable. Sadly, Patsy then Spotty had gone over the Rainbow Bridge before he died. At least they were not farmed out to someone else to care for them when Margretta moved.

Before my mother's father died, my mother's thirty-four-year-old brother, Arnett, came to visit his parents in Clifton. Just out of the Army where he had been stationed in Alaska for years, he was attempting to get his life back together. He had been married, was recently divorced, and was now a jobless single with few prospects in this factory-heavy city. Slim, always pleasant, and smiling, he was colorful to look at. He had blue eyes, pinkish skin, and wavy flaming red hair and eyebrows. I had seen him infrequently—and hardly knew him—yet the last time we met, he gave me a square-cut garnet ring. I didn't know why he did it, but I was overwhelmed at his generosity and thoughtfulness.

His parents were delighted to see him again after so long. He was my grandmother's favorite, calling him "Sonny." On the third summer's day of his short visit home, he had gone into the bathroom to take a cooling bath. There was no air conditioning in this old building. My grandmother had gotten his favorite lunch of fried liver and onions, with mashed potatoes and gravy, boiled summer squash, and tomatoes fresh from the garden ready for him. She was surprised he hadn't come out yet. She knocked and knocked, calling to him, "Lunch, Sonny." But there was no response.

After a few more minutes, she knocked harder, paused, and opened the door with trepidation. There, to her horror, she found him in the tub, dead. His head hung to the side, just above the bath water. She called my grandfather and the police. The coroner listed the cause of death as a heart attack. But he was only thirty-four! It nearly devastated his parents. Then when my grandfather followed suit, Margretta was sent into a tailspin. That was how she finally ended up with us. She went the frying pan into a raging bonfire.

Too often I did terrible things for what I thought were good reasons at the time. My mother's mother and father never had very much but were helpful whenever they could be. They had let my mother, brother, and me stay a week while my father was off on a business trip to Texas. He was working for a leather goods company. We had no place else to go. When my father came to pick us up, he treated my grandmother and grandfather coolly, as if they were invisible. Then to demonstrate his true feelings for them, he gave my mother, brother, and me gifts in front of them, with nothing for them.

As we were leaving, my grandmother slipped me a five-dollar bill. She wanted me to have it but I knew how much they needed it. Besides, I felt so bad about my father's dramatic slight of them.

Again I did the unthinkable. I surreptitiously left it behind on the dining room table. When she discovered it, she was furious. I should have taken her generous gift because she truly wanted me to have it. If I had given it some consideration at the time, I could probably have thought of a way to give it back to her somehow, in some form, a little later on. But I was thinking more about me and my guilt in taking it from her than about her generous feelings in giving it.

Maybe I was finally getting it. It was important not to spoil someone's altruism, irrespective of their financial situation. It was their decision to give their gift. I had no right to judge whether they should or not. It was a hard lesson for me to learn and stick to.

CHAPTER 28

Battling His Self-Sabotage

All along my father was showing progressively more aberrant behaviors. Yet we were continuing to take them in stride and make excuses—as in, "that was just the way he acted." When things happened slowly, we tended to accommodate to them, even providing explanations for them, no matter how strange they became. After my grandmother had left, we rented another apartment, on Henry Street in Framingham. His tobacco consumption increased to three packs a day. He always had a burning cigarette in hand. This was despite my increasing pulmonary distress with the particulate matter in the air. He never even seemed to notice even as I asked him not to smoke and told why. My coughing, gasping, and headaches simply made no impression on him.

Soon he began to stretch out on the sofa and sleep all day seemingly immobilized by depression. But his still burning cigarettes between his fingers were dropping hot ashes on his shirt, the rug, and the sofa, creating a fire hazard. Then he soon began ignoring his personal hygiene. This meant my mother and I had to wrest his increasingly odiferous soiled clothes from him, scrub them by hand, then take them to the Laundromat three miles away. With him permanently ensconced on the sofa, we couldn't invite anyone over to visit. There was no place else in which to "entertain" in this small two-bedroom, living room-dining room combination location even if there weren't the constant blue haze.

My K.H. would have snatched his burning cigarette from him and pointed out, "You are falling asleep with these cigarettes still burning, with hot ash all over the place. You are putting *everyone's* life at risk from a fire. Maybe you don't care about yourself, but you have to care about your family and the family that lives in the apartment upstairs." Then she would demand he do something about it ... right now!

To keep himself company he bought a blue parakeet in a cage. But it died several weeks later, undoubtedly from the tobacco smoke. I did another bad thing for what seemed like a good reason at that moment. Since my father seemed to be barely hanging on, I quickly found a look-alike replacement for his bird and never told him what I'd done. I felt he needed the bird. But I put another little bird in harm's way for him. I hated myself for doing that. The little bird didn't deserve this. My K.H. would not have gotten another bird. Instead, she would have let my father see what had happened as a result of his irresponsibility in polluting the indoor air.

Developing acute and increasingly frequent throbbing headaches at that time, my mother would sit in her bedroom in the dark squeezing her head in her hands, crying uncontrollably. I tried to get her to talk to me to tell me what was wrong and how I could help. She said there was nothing I could do. It was obvious she was in great pain and she wasn't just over-stressed and depressed. I told her we'd see a doctor as soon as she was able.

That was when my father stuck his nose in it, allegedly showing concern for her. He said he felt it was necessary to take me aside to tell me, "You are the one responsible for the stress she is under. You are the one giving her those debilitating headaches." He looked seriously at me, showing concern. "Look at your poor mother. She's in the bedroom suffering because you haven't been helping her. She's crying because you have been such a disappointment to her. You've been so thoughtless, thinking only about yourself, your needs and your wants. You need to think about her for a change. You need to think about all she has done for you. You need to help her around here. She can't do everything by herself!" Like me, my K.H. would have ignored his baseless accusations. Being irrational, he was hip-deep in denial. Nothing said to him by either of us would have made any difference to him.

Finally I was able to help my mother walk slowly to a doctor two blocks away to get a diagnosis. It was simple. Her blood pressure was 200+ over 165, putting her in danger of an imminent stroke or a heart attack. Consequently, she was very lucky to have seen him when she did. Once on medication, her headaches began to subside and she felt physically and emotionally better, considering her living circumstances.

Even with my mother as a model for dealing with his high blood pressure, my father chose not to follow her. He too had frequent headaches and had had them for a long time. He used uncoated aspirin—lots of it—instead. This added to his problems by burning holes in his stomach's lining.

Unexpectedly my father switched gears again and slipped into another cycle of grandiosity with lots of great new plans that couldn't fail for making him money. He was off the sofa, wanting to buy a new car and move into a new house. He wanted to locate a realtor and start looking right away, taking my mother with him. He had an idea for plastic phone book covers with advertising on them as well as a place to list important personal numbers on the front. Acting on his plan, he solicited ads and actually put out one cover which the post office delivered for him. But then things trailed off again and there were no more covers or anything else for one reason or another.

Increasingly my mother and I were acknowledging that there was something very wrong going on. But, of course, my father wouldn't or couldn't recognize it much less go to a doctor of any kind about it. Like every other service provider that existed, doctors were, in his estimation, useless because he knew more than they did. Moreover, you couldn't trust them. He knew his blood pressure was galloping in the stroke-out range but, he could manage it—without medication. He never wanted to feel dependent on anything, even though he already was deeply dependent on everyone and everything in every respect. That was his way to demonstrate what little control he had over his life.

Well over two hundred pounds now with elevating blood pressure, he was having trouble fitting into his clothes. He purchased a diet product called *Dietene*. However, instead of using it as a substitute for his regular meals, he used it in addition to them, further increasing his weight. He reported the product was no "damned good because it doesn't work." I couldn't help thinking he really knew what reality was but couldn't admit his contribution to the problem. That would make him less than "perfect." Both my K.H. and I ignored his complaints.

Illness was felling him more and more frequently. It could be stomach virus or bronchial congestion. He even fainted one time while on the toilet, requiring my mother to find a way to hoist him up to get him to the sofa before I arrived home from work at Massachusetts Institute of Technology. The only time he would take medication was when we forced it on him. But then he took it *only* until he felt a little better. He never finished the prescriptions, putting himself at greater risk for a relapse or something worse. His idea of control and independence often seemed at odds with common sense.

Over the years I had found that my father couldn't agree with me on anything I said or did. He always looked at it in a contradictory way which I suspected was on purpose. Later I wondered if he had actually agreed with me, would that make him "unacceptable" too. When we were driving south on North Main Street in Natick, we encountered a situation that would strongly test my contention.

Shortly after we had passed an old woolen mill on the right, I saw a young woman sitting on the left side of the road, intruding dangerously into the narrow two-lane street. At the edge of a gravel driveway where it met the paved road, she was convulsed in unrelenting grief. Just a foot beyond her to her right on the street was the body of a large, long-haired white cat. I had my father pull off the road to the right so we weren't blocking traffic. I jumped out of the car.

Once across the street, I sat beside her but back two feet so I was in no danger of being hit unless some car came into the driveway itself. I began talking with her to find out what had happened. But she wasn't listening. Her brain and heart were on the street with the cat. Then I tried something else, "You must love that cat a great deal to be staying with it." I noticed a flicker of recognition. I needed to get her back up the driveway to a less hazardous place. She was going to be road kill unless I could get her to move back.

With no cars coming, I carefully moved the still-warm cat's body up the drive—near her but a little farther back. If she wanted to be closer to the cat, she had to move back a bit herself. She told me, "Snowball was a neighborhood cat. I loved him with all my heart. He and I spent all our time together. He was so sweet, so gentle, and very smart. He meant more to me than my life." It was obvious what she was thinking. "I want to sit right here." She was in imminent peril. "I don't care if I'm hit by a car too. At least I'd be with Snowball."

She let out a deep-throated wail and cried all the harder. I put my arm around her. After about five minutes of gently rocking her, she calmed herself but tears were still rolling down her face, dripping off her chin. Focusing on Snowball, I tried to re-direct her attention. I said, "You know, it's up to you to give Snowball an appropriately loving send-off. You loved each other. He needs you now. But you can't do that for him if you let yourself be splattered all over the road by a car. It's up to you—and *only* you. *You* are the one who can keep your beloved friend's memory alive."

She was now regarding me more intently. This was when I finally persuaded her to move two feet further up the drive. She was now beside Snowball, gently stroking him, and in a safe place. Then I discussed with her ways she might honor her friend. I said, "You could make a coffin for him and put in it toys, flowers, and catnip he liked. You could put in a picture of you and him." She nodded, starting to get into the flow. We discussed all she could do. She was contributing ideas as well.

She said, "But, I'll never forget what happened to him today."

"No," I replied, getting ready to leave, "of course, you won't. But he would not want you to remember him at that one brief moment of his death and continue to mourn for him. He would want you to remember all the good times you had together—to celebrate all the joy, the silly things he did, all the tricks he could do. But most of all, how he showed you how much he loved you."

"Yes, yes." She showed some tear-stained enthusiasm. "I want Snowball to know he's in my heart and always will be." When she tried to smile, I smiled back and embraced her.

"He'll always be in your heart and mind. Nothing can ever erase that. That's how you'll keep him with you ... forever. So tell Snowball for me how lucky he is to have you." She smiled a heart-filling smile. With the two of them out of danger I said good-bye, re-crossed the street, got back in the car, and left, waving to her.

157

My father dramatically shook his head as he drove. His only comment was, "That was a stupidly dangerous thing to do. You could have been killed ... and for what? There was nothing you could do for the cat." My eyes rolled heavenward. We had neither the same perspectives nor the same values. While my K.H. could have stared him down as she explained it all to him, she more likely would have just shaken her head at his seeming disengagement from empathy and humanity.

CHAPTER 29

Risking Divorce

With my assistance my mother finally started divorce proceedings against my father. During their separation, he preyed upon her for all kinds of help from packages of Kraft Macaroni and Cheese to bread to toilet paper to soap and toothpaste to money. When what he truly "desired" was not forthcoming, he wrote her a stunning letter. She read it to her co-worker and me in the back room at the dress shop. He stated, "I could rape you if I wanted. I have rights as a husband ... and one of them is sexual access to you as my wife."

He sounded desperate and slightly unhinged. I was very concerned for my mother's safety. It immediately brought to mind the frightening plight of a next door neighbor to us on Main Street in Millis. Jill had befriended my mother and confided in her. She was planning to leave her husband who was constantly battering her. She was scared for her life. Then on the advice of her lawyer she finally did leave.

However, in a testosterone-infused rage, her husband, Arlen, searched for her, found her in a motel, and raped her making her pregnant. Because she had no other place else to go, she reluctantly went back home to him. My mother was in no position to help with money or refuge. After that, we moved and neither my mother nor I heard from or about her again.

That was not a time when Jill could have availed herself of an abortion if she had wanted one and if her religion had allowed her such recourse. She had no one to give her any kind of support or help with resources. There existed no shelters for women fleeing from domestic abuse. My father at the time had expressed his empathy with the husband, not with the wife. I admit this shocked me but really should not have surprised me.

"After all," he said, "She moved out while her husband was at work, took her belongings and some of their furniture. When her husband arrived home, he found the house empty. What a shock! What she did to him was a terrible thing." I didn't counter with the reality of it. My K.H. would have asked him point-blank, "So you're saying it was okay for him to frequently beat her then rape her?" I strongly suspected he would have found a way to justify and support what I considered an unjustifiable and unsupportable Old Testament perception of the husband-wife relationship. Then after hearing his letter to my mother, I was sure he really believed it.

The divorce process was awkward and disheartening. On the plus side, my mother's lawyer liked her a lot and felt she had long been getting a raw deal. As a result, he charged her nothing for the divorce fee, instead putting his fee on my father who couldn't pay for his expenses much less for my mother's too. According to her lawyer, "That's his problem. He's received enough coddling already." There was more truth to that than poetry.

In Massachusetts at that time a divorce couldn't be obtained because of "irreconcilable differences." Instead, there had to be some kind of physical assault that had been witnessed. My father had been verbally and psychologically abusive to my mother for decades, but had never physically assaulted her.

However, when the time came, I dutifully sat in the courtroom in the witness chair, looking very prim, proper, and appropriately honest. I told the judge with a straight face the big fat lie everyone expected me to tell. "Yes, Your Honor, I saw my father throw a large glass ashtray at my mother."

It felt so wrong. What kind of system made you lie in court to legally separate two people who were badly mismatched and so incredibly miserable? No matter what my deeply-entrenched gripes were with him, I felt unclean saying what I did because I knew it to be untrue. My K.H. was practical and said, "Don't sweat the small change. The object is to get a divorce, period. If the system makes you lie to get it, you lie. "

Actually, his throwing an ashtray, without hitting her of course, would have been a whole lot kinder than his having crippled my mother's sense of worth. He left her doubting her every thought, her every decision. I was punishing myself needlessly but I still felt I needed to do it.

After my mother divorced him, my father just couldn't get it together. "Stability" was not in his vocabulary. For a while, he lived in his old gray, rusting-out clunker Oldsmobile. I had no idea where he got it. My mother provided him periodically with some more of life's basics.

There was one thing enlightening about my father's situation. I could easily see how under the right circumstances *anyone* could become homeless and have difficulty recovering. All anyone needed was to have something major happen in life that removed the social and/or financial support system. Of course, that wasn't what happened to my father. He had had years of opportunities and support but his situation was a series of life events with which he did not and, maybe could not, cope.

The next thing we knew he had disappeared. He turned up living with a woman in Western Massachusetts. No one had even suspected she existed. I wondered how long she had been in the picture. But it didn't really matter. It was sheer curiosity. After about six months, he left her to move to the southwest coast of Florida to work for Mickelson Brothers in real estate development on Marco Island.

When he had been able to step outside his homeless persona, he had made contacts in Massachusetts with Mickelson sales representatives. They had seen him as having potential for their sales crew. They sent him on several trips to Florida to interview which then sealed the deal. He worked out of the Massachusetts office for a while then moved to Florida. He was in. I thought good for him and hoped he would make the most of it.

He didn't. He continued to demonstrate that he couldn't keep a job for one reason or another. Over a matter of many months he felt he was being ripped off. Whether as a result of his erroneous perception or of reality, he began hurling accusations of backstabbing and commission stealing by his close sales associates who had been with the company longer. Hanging on as long as possible, he grudgingly left Mickelson. But he was still trying to collect what he claimed was owed him of his over-due commissions. He was in no position to sue even if suing had been the right course of action.

After several interim jobs, he began to work in a local eatery. While there, he kept up his running mental accounting of all that had gone wrong in his life, to which he alluded in his letters to me. Those victimizing events had left him now, could he even utter the phrase, a "short-order cook." He felt he had sunk as low as he could go.

CHAPTER 30

Missing the Big Picture

What was a crime was that my father was someone who was very bright and who had aced psychological and achievement tests for companies, looking so good that companies were concerned he might be lying about himself or somehow cheating on their tests. When they didn't hire him, he shook his head, "They didn't want to see how good I was. I probably threatened them." If only he had been savvier, he would have demonstrated himself to be psychometrically just a little less than "perfect." In that way he would have been accepted as "really good, but "somewhat' flawed," like everyone else there, and gotten the job. But he had to be seen as "perfect." His ego depended upon it.

Early on he had created several push and pull toys that were simple, unique, and delighted young children. One was a whale that waved its tail and opened its mouth as it rolled along to reveal Jonah on its tongue. Another was a duck with rubber "webbed" feet attached to the wheels so the feet would go slap, slap, slap as the duck moved. A large toy manufacturer bought his designs for $35 and then mass-produced and mass-marketed them, making big bucks from which my father did not benefit in the slightest.

He never forgot his being "screwed over" by them, as he put it, and never made another toy. He never let go of any perceived slight or real action against him. It never occurred to him to continue making his wooden toys, his primary creative outlet, but learn more about contracts. Or, better still, he could have hired a contract lawyer. Instead, he cavalierly dismissed the notion, "What would a *lawyer* know anyway that I don't already know? Lawyers! You know how *they* are. He would probably shaft me with billing for every little thing. No, I won't fall for their trap."

Shortly after becoming a short-order cook, he met someone he described to me in a letter as a "plain, little dumpling of a woman with a funny last name" and he married her. It seemed so sad to me that he started making excuses for his marrying her. Never once did he say he cared for her or was pleased to have her as a companion. He praised the friendliness and tricks of the little rescue dog he had acquired, "Sport," more than he acknowledged her values as a person.

He made it sound as if he had married as a last resort—as if he were desperate and she were the only one around. That struck me as so cruel to her. My hope was that he simply didn't want to compare her to my mother to me since his new wife would probably come out second-best attractiveness-wise in a competition from the way he described her. But physical attractiveness wasn't everything, though I suspect he probably thought it was. If he really felt that way about her, I hoped he didn't communicate that to her; but how could he not do so? My K.H. would have brought that to his attention, stating, "What you're saying about her sounds unkind. She obviously cares for you. You married her because you care, about something if not about her. You need to reconsider what you think about her because you're going to communicate it to her in some way. And I don't think you want to hurt her like that."

In truth, he really could no longer survive on his own. He was very lucky to have found someone. And maybe it didn't matter why she married him. Maybe she believed he had something positive to share with her, even if only friendship or a roof over her head. She certainly didn't marry him for his money, his stock portfolio, fancy car, or toy patents.

CHAPTER 31

Forging a New Life

Desperately in need of a change, my mother and I sold some of our possessions and pooled our money. We spruced up the old station wagon and traded it in for a slightly "newer" car. This was a pale blue Ford station wagon with faux-wood-cladding. With the car packed to the gunwales, we then packed and attached a small U-Haul, and headed for San Diego. Expected to be uneventful, the move was fraught with adventure we'd never have conceived experiencing.

On our way in the hot, dry, dusty Texas panhandle we pulled off the highway into a two-tank gas station with its attached beige-colored-stucco store for re-fueling. It was the only sign of life along vast stretches of only scrub and dirt for miles and miles. Standing by a beat-up red Chevy pickup truck in front of the store were two men in sweat-stained cowboy hats, faded jeans, and scuffed cowboy boots. With several days' whisker growth, they eyed us as we pulled in. Taking our measure, they talked between themselves.

Uncomfortable with their attention, I filled the gas tank without acknowledging their presence. Leaving my mother in the car, I walked to the store and quickly paid. Their continued interest was obvious as I gazed through the plate glass store window. I walked casually back to the car, still ignoring them. I didn't mention them to my mother for fear she would do something to let them know we had noticed them. She had a tendency to act before thinking, demonstrating provocative nonverbal behaviors, like staring, especially with men. Upon departing, I drove down a dirt road which I assumed was the re-entry access to the highway. But it wasn't. To my horror, it was a dead-end. There were twelve-inch-deep ditches on either side of the road. A barb wire greeted us all three sides. We were stopped cold.

My stomach did a series of flips. We were trapped—totally vulnerable—if those men decided to follow us. What have I done? I asked myself, shaking my head. I quickly alighted from the car to survey the actual space available in which to turn around. It was worse than I had could have imagined. If it had been only the car that had to be jockeyed to re-position us, that would have been an arduous but relatively simple process. But with the U-Haul as well which could easily move opposite of the car when backing up if one weren't careful turning the wheels—uh, oh, bad news!

What about trying to drive backward to ease out of the dirt road? As I looked at the distance involved, the curves, how it dipped in some places, and the effort it would take to keep both vehicles moving straight back, I dumped that notion. But we couldn't sit there. We couldn't wait for our attentive cowpokes to mosey along in our direction for a lip-smacking, "Howdy, ma'am."

Without a yardstick, I made multiple distance calculations. It was only the slightest possibility that we could turn around. That would require not dropping a trailer or car wheel into one of the ditches. My mother wanted to drive. I adamantly refused. I would do it. I had gotten us into this angst-ridden situation. Moreover, I felt I handled the U-Haul better than she did. I had had much more practice backing up. I knew this would be extremely touchy.

To my mother's dismay, I stationed her to the back and side of the trailer. She was to give me directions. Slowly I began backing and filling. Even with my driver's side window open, hearing my mother clearly was next to impossible. She shouted directions at me. It wasn't long before we were screaming at each other. It was getting more difficult to hear. We were gravely misunderstanding each other.

Frustration was growing. She shouted, "Left! No, not that left! It's my left, your right." Having turned the wheels the wrong way, I had to re-gain my former position. "Turn the wheel toward me now. No! Not that much. Okay, that's better. Try again, same direction with less turn. Whoa! Wait a minute. Let me check the other side. You're getting too close to the ditch on the other side. Pull forward about an inch. No! Not enough. A little bit more. That's enough. Now turn the wheel to the right. Crap. Now the other trailer wheel is too close to the other ditch."

Dust devils were swirling around us, coating our sweaty skin. The stress was telling on both of us both. We tried to temper our anger. But we shouted ever louder back and forth. We were getting hotter, sweatier, dustier, and thirstier. We kept on. Two inches forward and one inch back. I repeated that over and over. The trailer was slowly moving around us. Two inches forward and one inch back. Frequently we came within a cat's whisker of sinking over the side of the road.

I gave the barbed wire fencing a second thought. At this point I didn't care if we rubbed the trailer against the barbs. I didn't care if we dented the fence. I didn't care if we scratched all the paint off the trailer. I jumped out of the car. How flexible was this wire? A closer inspection of it gave me an "aha!" There actually was some slack in it. What if I could use that extra space beneath and beyond the wire? Could that give us a little extra latitude? The ditches stopped at the wire.

When I backed up the car, the trailer pushed against the barbed wire somewhat diagonally. It gave us a little more space in which to negotiate. Inches back. Turning left. Inches forward. Turning right. Inches back. My heart leapt in my chest. I think ... just maybe. Inches back. Turning left. Inches forward. Turning right. Please let this work! I hadn't wanted to give up. But our situation had looked very bleak. Once more forward. Back. Forward again. A little more back. Forward. Back.

Oh, my god! We had finally re-positioned ourselves enough to get back on the road. And, incredibly, we had not destroyed the barbed wire fence in the process. However, I was not about to feel guilty if we had. Both back in the car, we were soaked, dust-covered, and exhausted but joyous. We looked at each other, blinked hard to keep back well-deserved tears.

Grinning I said, "Great job! Okay. Now let's get the hell out of here!" With relief I dared not express to my mother, I noted there was still no sign of the beat-up red pickup ... or anyone else ... approaching us. Hours later when we had finally showered, had eaten, and were ensconced in a clean motel for the night, we slept well all night long.

After our finding an apartment at 4025 Arizona Street, off University, in San Diego, my mother secured a secretarial job at an electronics firm in La Jolla just north of us. I set up shop a few blocks farther north of that at what was then called the Scripps Clinic and Research Foundation. There I worked in the endocrinology department on a double-blind study of a diabetic medication from Upjohn Pharmaceuticals.

The first apartment we had checked out wouldn't accept us. The dour-looking fiftyish female apartment manager was sure we were lying about being mother and daughter.Looking us up and down, she said, "I think you're really sisters and are likely to have wild, loud parties bringing in all sorts of men." While I thought she was out of her mind, I tried to convince her otherwise. She wasn't having any part of it. That situation would be just plain "unacceptable to her quiet complex." It was gender discrimination pure and simple. But we needed a place to live more than we needed to initiate a gender discrimination law suit against her. Fortunately the manager at 4025 didn't question our familial relationship and welcomed us.

Scripps Clinic was perched high above the La Jolla Cove so you could hear the waves slamming into the rocks below, rumbling, exploding, and spraying out again. La Jolla was an attractive, somewhat elite little town, where celebrities lived year round or in seasonal homes. Many came to Scripps Clinic under film studio contracts for annual physicals. We stayed in the attractive San Diego-La Jolla area for a year and a half. Despite its being near the water, we sometimes baked in the summer. Winter inundated us with heavy rains. Surprisingly, we even had the briefest of snowfalls. It lasted perhaps ten minutes, melting before it hit the ground. But overall the climate was very temperate.

We enjoyed the gardens and museums at Balboa Park, attended singles' dances at the El Cortez Hotel, and went often to the famous San Diego Zoo and their Nature Park. While there, I also attended law classes at California Western School of Law after work at the clinic every day. Doing research in the law library until way after midnight, however, was hard going after a long day at work.

While San Diego boasted lots of sunshine and no icy roads or shoveling snow, the traffic was heavy and increasing. Moreover, orangey-brown smog was beginning to drift in over the Anza-Borrego Desert from Los Angeles. In spite of that we visited the desert frequently. But all in all, we felt enthusiastic we had found a home with great possibilities for a workable new life. There was so much to explore with San Diego as our hub. That was until we began experiencing a series of seriously discomforting safety situations.

It was at Scripps that I *didn't* experience my first earthquake. I was headed to the endocrinology research laboratory one floor below and in the next building. I had medication study reports to deliver so I took the elevator down. As I exited, there was palpable anxiety all around me. Clinical staff, secretarial, and research staff were milling around. Some hurriedly moved through. Some were inquiring of one another. Perplexed, I asked, "What's going on?"

"What? Didn't you feel the floor roll in waves? We just had an earthquake!"

"What? Are you kidding? I didn't feel a thing." They looked at me as if I were either crazy or insensate. "Where were you a few minutes ago?"

"I was just in the elevator coming down."

"Oh, well, that explains it. The elevator must have absorbed the shock. You really missed something. It must have been at least a four-point-five. I'll bet it hit L.A. with a six-point-zero or more. Well, I guess you just missed all the excitement. That means you'll have to wait a little longer to experience your 'Welcome-to-California' seismic event."

Oh, crap! I thought. Really? Was that the start of the scientifically-predicted *big* one that's already way behind? Dropping off the files, I returned to my office. My mother called, excited. She exclaimed, "Oh, boy! I was out mailing some packages when I almost fell off the sidewalk in the shaking. Remember in Long Beach the displaced sidewalk and the house that had been wrenched off its foundation? Do you think there are going to be more quakes here soon? Maybe after-shocks? Or maybe stronger primary ones? We'll have to be sure to catch a meteorological report tonight." That thought discomforted both of us. We became hyper-aware of any untoward motion or loud deep noise.

Then one sunny Sunday in the late afternoon we were driving back from Los Angeles. We had visited the Griffith Park and Observatory and the Huntington Library art collections and botanical gardens. Suddenly we collided with a concrete wall of fog. We were approaching Oceanside, heading south on Interstate 5. It was unlike anything we had ever encountered before in Massachusetts. This looked and felt solid even as we slowly slid into it.

It was getting dark. But we were enshrouded in a dense, ominous whiteness. Strangely cars were whizzing by us. I felt both amazed and befuddled. They were passing us at high speeds. We were crawling because we couldn't see. How could they do that? Do they have some special light to cut through the fog that we don't have? I could see no more than ten feet in front of me, just beyond the hood of the car. And yet traffic was literally zooming by. As we slowly slunk by Carlsbad, our tensions rose by the moment.

Traffic was always heavy and moving along at a fast clip on I-5. But this was incomprehensible. Becoming more anxious, I contemplated pulling over to the side of the road. Perhaps we could wait for the fog bank to lift. But we had no way of knowing how these things behaved. Did they last for twenty minutes or eight hours? Pulling over might get us struck from behind by a high-speed car. There was no question. We had to keep moving. But our creeping along was also likely to get us in an accident. We seemed to be the only car not chewing up the highway at sixty miles per hour or more. Our choices were now slim to none.

My neck and shoulders ached from the strain. My eyes burned. They were becoming blurry. I was getting a headache. So I made a proposal to my mother. She was already gripping the dashboard in a stranglehold. Her face was drained of color as she peered out into the blanket which had wrapped itself around us. I offered a suggestion, "Let's pick the next vehicle that pulls in front of us. We'll ride its taillights at whatever speed it moves." Neither one of us was happy about the extreme danger involved. This portended a body-crushing, blood splattering accident in our future. But this was whether we did nothing or plunged ahead. So we agreed to take our chances. Calmly we resigned ourselves to possibly not making it.

A line of tail-gating cars raced by us. No one cut in front of us. Come on, come on! I mentally shouted at them. My throat was tightening. Minutes went by. The vice on my temples was tightening. My neck was stiffening. I didn't believe it!

Then a large, open-back farm truck swerved sharply in front of us. Its taillight was detectable at ten feet. My heart thumped wildly. I shoved the accelerator to the floor, pinning us back against our seats. I shouted, "Mother, hang on!" She had already rammed her feet nearly through the carpeting, locking her knees. We almost kissed the truck's bumper as we flew along behind it. Every minute we risked its suddenly stopping short or careening into another vehicle.

For the next forty-five minutes we blindly roared down the invisible highway. We clung to that wood-slat and metal vision of hope. It would either get us home ... or get us killed. My cramped thigh and calf muscles screamed for me to take my foot off the gas and relax. My left foot was shoved into the floor, nearly elevating me off my seat. No. I wouldn't let the truck get away from us no matter what. It was our savior.

I checked the fuel gauge. It was at half of a tank. Please, please, please let this pea soup thin out so we can know when we arrive. I shook my head and chuckled to myself, "when" we arrive? What was it Emily Dickinson said about "hope"? "Hope is the thing with feathers that perches in the soul and sings the tune without words and never stops at all." I could see its ruffled feathers as hope peered out of my sub-consciousness.

The farm truck continued its NASCAR laps straight ahead. We moved farther south. The fog began to thin. Something ... something ... not quite sure what it was up ahead. A highway sign? Was it that for our exit? I squinted, straining my eyes. I couldn't tell for sure. It was coming up fast. I'd have to act immediately if it turned out to be ours. The moment I could make out the misty letter "U-N-I-V," I turned the wheel sharply to the right. Still going sixty mph, I took the exit. The tires squealed. The rear of the car skidded to the left. It barely missed the steel guardrail. But we were finally on University.

It was a moment to celebrate as we slowed our speed. We were moving toward Arizona Street. The fog was lessening incrementally. And soon there was our apartment building. I was never so overjoyed to see our apartment again. This was the first time I had relaxed and let my mind wander. I took a moment to wonder if I ever wanted to risk our heading north again by car. How often was that fog likely to happen? It all left me feeling very uneasy. I looked up and saw hints of stars above the mist. We were safe now unless the earth began to shake again. We'd been tempered in two crucibles and come out stronger. The second shoe had dropped. Will that be the last? Could there be something else? Does San Diego get hurricanes? Tornadoes? Tsunamis? Floods? We asked ourselves how many more times could we tempt fate like that and still make it through.

After we parked on the street, we dragged our bodies on wobbly, cramped-muscled legs up the stairs to number ten. We collapsed. Our minimally-padded cot bed mattresses felt like heavenly clouds. Our heads were now throbbing, eyes tearing, and shoulder muscles going into spasm. Only sleep could cure our state of total mental and physical exhaustion. But still something was nibbling at the edge of my dreams. It was a nagging sense that this was not what we had bargained on when we moved here. Were things going to finally even off over time?

Fears and uncertainty had suddenly attacked us both. We had had such high hopes for remaining here but this strange turn of events gave us pause. Maybe this was a fluke and the end of it. But unfortunately that was not so. We still had one more major challenge to encounter which would set in stone our desire to stay or go.

That September downed power lines sparked a conflagration in eastern San Diego County in Kitchen Creek near the Cleveland National Forest. This was an area recorded as having such fires every ten years or so. Fueled by the notorious hot, dry Santa Ana winds it kindled the dry, flammable chaparral, sage scrub, and manzanita. It rapidly progressed west, reportedly covering thirty miles in only twenty-four hours. Called the "Laguna Fire" because it occurred in the Laguna Mountains, the disaster became later-known as the third-largest fire in California history. It consumed over 175,000 acres, nearly four hundred homes, killed fourteen people, and totally devastated two communities.

According to hourly news reports tracking the firestorm, it moved closer and closer to San Diego. Gusting winds spread it north and south as well as if to begin to surround us on three sides. Segments of Interstate 8, which runs east-west through the Cleveland National Forest area, were melting. Anything in the fire's path was incinerated. The excited blaze devoured ever more acreage as it continued its progress toward the city.

The skies to the east looked inflamed. Oranges melded into reds. The hot air hit you as if from a blast furnace. It was nearly impossible to breathe. Like snow, ash was falling everywhere. The small pine tree in a terra cotta pot on our second-floor balcony was covered with it, giving it a deathly pall. The apartment complex pool resembled a witch's cauldron of coal tar. When the ash struck our car, it created basic pH burn splotches in its paint job.

I thought if only it would rain heavily, it might suffocate the fire. But that hope was shattered. I learned that the rains could not be heavy enough to dampen the fire. The heat would evaporate the precipitation before it reached the fire and the ground. Asked to avoid driving outside the city so as not to interfere with firefighters and their equipment, my mother and I stayed home from work for a few days. Making it worse, firefighters could not use the aircraft and fire retardant they often depended upon. The winds were too heavy.

With the windows open or closed it was like an inferno in our apartment. There was no air-conditioning in the complex. Not being prepared for wildfires in Massachusetts, we had no floor fan, humidifier, or air purifier. We had missed the necessity of adding that to our new California safety kit.

There was nothing to make our apartment more livable. Instead, we lay on the beige-carpeted floor with wet cloths over our mouths and noses. Just standing up to re-wet the cloth, get a drink of water, or use the bathroom was like being slammed in the face with a steaming rock from a sauna.

My eyes, sinuses, and throat felt seared from the heat. My chest felt heavy. And I immediately began to feel faint. We had to crawl to wherever we wanted to go. But mostly, it felt too onerous to move.

Neither of us moved unless it was an emergency. We drank water constantly. We ate off the linoleum floor of the kitchen ... when we actually felt like eating. We doused our heads. We even put wet sheets on the kitchen floor on which to sleep. They dried too quickly to be much help.

By the time the fires were mostly contained in the east, in a little over a week, we had sadly come to the conclusion that we were no longer ready for San Diego. It was all too much at once. After the earthquake, smothering fog, and strangling fire, we were felt we needed to go elsewhere. Where? Back to Massachusetts? My K.H. said, "Wait. It's been a rocky start but you can wait a while longer. This place holds more opportunities for you than back east." But it felt like too much all at once. We were both sad to go and yet relieved. As soon as we could, we rented another small U-Haul trailer and packed it and the car. We were about to embark on another pricey cross-county trip. When the second week of October arrived, we started back.

As we approached El Cajon we could only crawl, rumbling over the undulating, often severely buckled, asphalt surface of I-8. When we entered the more heavily-burned area, we passed blackened trees, junipers, chamisa, prickly pear and cholla cactus. The stench of charred bodies of hapless animals overcame us. Destroyed homes could still be seen smoldering. The road finally smoothed out again. Our express vehicle devoured the miles east to propel us to safety and our former "refuge." In the back of my mind was the thought that we hadn't given southern California the chance it deserved to beguile us to stay. I didn't really want to go back to Massachusetts. But at that moment, with flames nearly licking our boots, I didn't care. I didn't believe in "signs" but the rapid succession of those events was too much to ignore given our previous mindset.

CHAPTER 32

Heading Back

As we rolled back northeast, my six-foot-four brother, Wally, who had left the Navy, had already moved to Florida. He was now living south of Naples, near Marco Island. He was working on a fishing boat in the Gulf of Mexico. That is, he was fishing when he wasn't riding his used Harley like a .357 Magnum bullet tearing up the asphalt on County Road 92 to the east. My father was pleased to have my brother in the vicinity. It gave him the opportunity to claim some sense of family connection which he desperately needed as he repeatedly demonstrated in his letters to me.

But that connection was not to be the sweet end of the lollypop as he had hoped. My brother too had suffered at the hands of his father. As a result, he knew to keep his father at arm's length for the most part to protect himself. Wally associated with and used him only when he deemed it necessary. He had managed something I had yet to pull off.

Wally had been penalized over the years by my father's constantly comparing him to me academically. It didn't matter that I was compelled to do well in school to get my rewards that way. Of course, my brother had always blamed *me* for it. Hanging on to whatever parent-child bond he thought existed, he couldn't bring himself to blame his father for anything. That was too threatening for him. He didn't want to abandon his parent and, in turn, be abandoned by him. As he had learned from his father, his mother didn't count. She would always be there for him. But so what? His father was the one with the power to give acceptance— or withhold it.

Consequently, one day back in Millis when Wally had had enough of being disapproved of grade-wise by his father, he shouted at me in the driveway, red-faced, all but crying, "You think you're such a hot shit. But you're nothing but a cold turd." That pretty well summed up our cooling relationship from there on out. But, as fate would have it, we never got the chance to revisit our siblinghood to see if we could salvage anything positive from it.

Just before Christmas in 1969, December 17 to be exact, my mother and I received a call from the Florida Coast Guard. My mother and I were living together in an apartment on Winthrop Street in Framingham. This was to make our once-again-meager paychecks go further. Besides she still didn't feel strong enough to make it on her own. Always on the margins, having only five dollars in cash in her pocket for gas, she used our station wagon to drive to her sales job.

I walked several block to work at Bangor Rivets Company on Waverly Street where I was a secretary. I loathed being a secretary. I still had pretensions of becoming a physician. Moreover, I found the work boring and more than a little crazy-making. The aging, rotund owner felt it acceptable to presume to pat my behind with a laugh in front of customers on their way out to their three-martini lunch. If my eyes could have poisoned him, he would have already been writhing on the floor. It didn't faze him one bit. It was one of the perks of being the owner. He just laughed again. My K.H. could have generated a more meaningful response. But that would have gotten me fired. But when that happened, it would have been a "so what!"

The owner had put his non-business-oriented son in as a titular company president. He seemed nonplussed most of the time, signing documents given him by his father. The marketing manager, the one for whom I worked mostly, had blatantly shown his interest in having an extra-marital affair with me. I said, "No thanks," but he wasn't one to give up so easily. He seemed sure I couldn't resist his "charm."

Consequently, late one evening he came by my apartment complex to demonstrate the full range of his alluring qualities. Several sheets to the wind, he planted himself beneath our second-floor apartment window, singing at the top of his lungs, "I Can't Give You Anything But Love, Baby." Then he called in my direction, "Come on out. Come on out and talk to me, you little cutie. Kelly wants you!"

His taking his shirt off in an uncoordinated strip tease suggested his pants wouldn't be far behind.

I would have loved to have ignored him, assured my neighbors would call the police. But I felt that option was rife with problems since I needed to keep my job a while longer. But, maybe I was fooling myself. Maybe I was really afraid to act. My K.H. said, "Let him do his dumbest and be picked up by the police. You don't have to get involved. It won't affect your job." I wasn't so sure.

Setting my jaw and breathing deeply, I went down the stairs and out front. I hoped I could temporarily pacify him or, at the very least, get him to button his lip. "But, baby," he slurred, trying to put his hands on my shoulders to steady himself, "you know I need you. I really need you. How about just a little." He made a grab for my breast. I pushed his hand away, upsetting his balance. He landed on one knee on the grass in the bright illumination of the security light at the glass front door. "Come on. How about a little smooch? We can hide behind the bushes here so no one will see us." Still on one knee, he tried to put his hand on my inner thigh. Begging, he whispered, "How about a little blow job? I'll give you something good in return. How about it, huh? We could always go back to my place. My wife's away."

I shoved him hard into a sitting position. "Kelly, I told you 'no' and I meant 'no.' The police are probably on their way to pick you up. It's 10:30 at night. You loudly serenaded this entire building. I want you to leave. Right now ... get in your car. Go home."

I hoped he'd be arrested for a DUI but not injure anyone before that. "I'll forget what happened tonight *if* you don't try this again. But I definitely won't forget it, if you do!" The next day at work, behind his closed door, I spoke firmly with a more sober and subdued Kelly. A repeat performance *would* come back to bite him in the butt with a vengeance. He agreed. He let it go, never again trying for either a sloppy or non-sloppy seduction.

To add to Bangor Rivets' dysfunctional family, the heavy-set accountant, whose office was across from mine, always seemed disgruntled about everything. He was likewise invariably under the weather. He kept a bottle of Old Crow in his lower left-hand desk drawer. More often than not, he came to work bleary-eyed, puffy-faced, and reeking of bourbon. He couldn't stop complaining acrimoniously about his wife. She just didn't understand his deep and abiding thirst.

When he stumbled, nearly falling as he tried to get out of his chair to take some documents to the general manager's office, I asked if I could help. He looked at me blankly, licking his lips as if his mouth were dry. He threw his head back to see me better then leaned forward with his face in mine, and said, "You wouldn't understand. Nobody understands. My life is so unfair." Then he bounced off the door jamb to disappear into the hall. He staggered in the direction of the manager's office.

Two days later everyone but the rivet makers and I left on vacation for a week to ten days. This had been made known to me. But what I hadn't expected was that Doris, the wife of the manufacturing supervisor, who handled all the orders, invoices, filing, and shipping, also had to hurriedly leave for an indeterminate period of time. Her husband, who had just had a serious heart attack on the manufacturing floor below, needed full-time care.

Every product-related task other than the manufacturing itself had been dropped unceremoniously into my lap to perform. I was to continue my regular secretarial duties, which were minimal in everyone's absence, plus take phone and mail orders, deal with customer complaints about shipping, create and file invoices, and keep accounting records. Then I was to make sure everything was shipped and shipped properly through the appropriate freight lines which I likewise had to schedule.

Thoughtfully, Doris had created time, while someone gave her a respite, to give me a quick course in what I needed to do. But I didn't feel comfortable handling it all, much less doing so with ease. Besides, I didn't want to. After nearly a week, I was at the end of my tether. I knew I wasn't doing all the things that I should be doing. I was not sure what I did do that was right. Furthermore, I didn't give a damn. I knew I had to find something else and soon. My K.H. would have said "to hell with it," sent the manager a telegram stating she was leaving, and then left. This was above and beyond the call of duty. Besides, no one had offered me any "hazardous duty pay."

The young Coast Guard person on the phone stated, "The fishing boat on which Wally worked had foundered in the Gulf during a bad storm. The Coast Guard sent out a rescue helicopter. It picked up all crew members. But, then, it somehow crashed into the water. All those aboard had been killed." My mother was rendered mute, inconsolable.

She had wanted so much more for her son. It was especially so now that he was less attached to his controlling father. As much as she hurt from his years of negative behavior towards her, including his not having communicated with her since my father went to Florida, she forgave him. She claimed, "It was really his father's fault. Besides, Wally did what he did to survive." I wasn't quite so sanguine about that explanation. I felt he too should have been held accountable for his actions and their consequences.

She would have loved for him to have gone back to college—but *not* in business as his father had directed before—in something he truly liked. But she didn't try to push him into it. If he wanted to fish for a living, he could fish. He was bright, had a high IQ, and had potential if he wanted to explore it. All she wanted was for him to finally be happy in all aspects of his life. But all that ended at age twenty-four.

Now what would she do? Have a funeral or memorial for him? We weren't particularly religious. She didn't know and that pained her. But in our poverty-like state again—we'd made considerably more in California with the type of work we were doing—we didn't have the wherewithal for her to travel to Florida. The road trip back to Massachusetts had sapped our accumulated funds. The car, having developed *problems since San Diego, might not get her there even if she* could have handled the gas and other travel expenses. We surely couldn't afford a round-trip plane ticket.

As if history were repeating itself, it was the same problem when my mother's mother, died of a heart attack on a Greyhound bus heading to Oregon. She was going to live with her old girlfriend, Torhild, after leaving us. We couldn't arrange anything for her much less get her possessions. They had been placed in storage in New Jersey before moving in with us. There were photos, letters, and personal things of hers and my mother's father we wanted. Worse, on

179

the bus she had been stripped of her watch and wedding rings. Even those few personal objects were beyond our reach.

But now what would be done for Wally? Somehow my father, despite his similarly fragile financial status, took care of the "arrangement." He never shared any of that with us. We decided not to inquire about any of the details. I suspected my father was able to sell Wally's Harley to handle the expenses for whatever he did.

CHAPTER 33

Binding Ties That Strangle

In spite of everything, my father and I had kept up communication by letter. While I still felt the sadness about my unrequited paternal love in childhood, I no longer felt the need to seek my father's acceptance as an adult. That is not to say that I still did not feel "unacceptable" in general as a result. But now he provoked in me a hate-tinged pity and compassion. This was when he would tell me that he could send letters only once in a while because he didn't have the paper, envelopes, or stamps. He always knew where to place the blade between my ribs and twist. How much of what he said was true and how much was a manipulated semblance of the truth to pluck the heart strings? I didn't know.

I felt I *had* to give him a family safety rope to hang on to. At the same time, I knew in doing that I was risking looping that rope around my own neck, perhaps hanging myself with it. He was a poisonous influence. I was not yet immune to his toxicity. I needed to believe I *could* let go when I was ready. But unlike my K.H., who would have let him be hoisted on his own petard, painfully I couldn't pinpoint when that would be.

Soon the realization came to me via my K.H. that I had to concede that all that had happened in my life that was associated with my father was *past*. It was all over. There was no way I could go back to alter it. I could do not a single thing to change those events or their impact. Remembering all the wrongs I felt that had been done me and getting angry all over again was just plain dumb. I had to stop for my own sake. As I was discovering, there was nothing like self-pity to thoroughly dissipate a person.

I had to accept that my ongoing blame and ensuing anger would not affect my father one bit. Blame and anger would hurt only me. I was raising my blood pressure and getting symptoms of an ulcer. By constantly regurgitating the pain and guilt, I wasn't solving the problem. I wasn't even trying. I was keeping it going. And bemoaning the fact that I was being foolish didn't make me any smarter. It just gave me something else to complain about.

I needed to let the safety line go or handle my father in a more detached, less emotional fashion. I needed to step back. I needed to become objective, to analyze the situation that I was allowing to ruin my life. I needed to change what I could and let the rest go. I needed to let go of the hate but let the pity and compassion remain.

Since I had gotten a secondary education teaching certificate along the way, my father thought I *should* be teaching. As a result, he continually sent me applications from surrounding school systems in Florida. I figured he did it to effect two things he wanted: (1) have me near him and (2) have me away from my mother whom he still resented for "having made him a miserable failure."

With him seemingly enjoying his getting these forms for me, I decided not to tell him how much I really disliked teaching high school at that time. I had been instructing in English at a high school in Framingham. This was when significant changes were brewing in the school's attitudes about students. The atmosphere had taken a turn for the somewhat *laissez-faire*.

Students were being given freedoms to act more like adults as if they were mature enough to handle them. The sentiment of society suggested we had to allow students to express themselves more and be less structured with them. The only problem with that was that the students were expressing themselves by doing as they pleased. They were essentially flipping a finger at any authority figure they chose, including us teachers.

One time a female student was working on a large macramé piece as I lectured on "Ivanhoe." When I asked her to please put it away, she balked, "I'm not disturbing anyone by doing it so I will if I want to." That did not please me. I responded calmly, "While you may not be disturbing your classmates, your working on your macramé is distracting to me and my providing you with this lesson which is part of the upcoming test. So please put it away."

With students testing their wings, pushing the envelope, and tending to go overboard in doing so, I became tired of constantly encountering those "I will if I want to" situations. I had encountered enough of those in my personal life. I was not willing to tolerate them in my job as well. Having students dare me to object to whatever they were doing in order to provoke me was not what I was teaching for. Too often I heard, "Send me to the principal's office if you want. They don't want me there. You're supposed to deal with it." It was like trying to communicate with two-year-olds who had just discovered the power of the word "no."

Trying to squeeze some useful educational material in between the annoying, manipulative interactions didn't sit well with my temperament. Incivility was beginning to run rampant. I felt that if I treated students with respect, I expected them to treat me with respect in return.

As far as I was concerned, they could enjoy exhibiting their acquisition of power on someone else's watch. Teaching psychology to college students, which I did later on, was much more satisfying. This was especially true of those in the School of Fine Arts at Boston University. They showed maturity, discipline, and responsibility, unlike many of the students in B.U.'s College of Liberal Arts.

A soldier in Vietnam to whom I had been writing responded abruptly to my mentioning my leaving the high school. He told me, "Get off your dead ass and do what you are supposed to do. Suck it up and get back in there and teach them anyway" In other words, I was to teach them no matter how I felt about their behavior. I didn't take his unsolicited "sage" advice. My K.H. cheered me on for not returning because I felt guilty. She suggested I tell the soldier to stuff his opinion.

At that time I had been writing to thirty individuals in combat. This was the result of a request by the USO, (the Congressionally-chartered, private, non-profit United Services Organizations, for anyone willing to correspond with soldiers. I sent my picture and a short bio to them which they displayed. I was inundated with notes from those who were stressed, traumatized, scared, lonely, and in need of some warm connection from "home." They needed comfort when they weren't being shot at or "fragged" by hand grenades. To keep up with two letters a week to each person, I "patriotically" washed and re-used stamps. This went on for many months.

Some soldiers were so thankful to me for my friendly letters and concern for them that they proposed marriage. One who had received six Purple Hearts in battle was already setting up couples' quarters for us at Fort Jackson in South Carolina. My K.H. and I had great difficulty responding as sensitively as possible with my regretful refusals. It made me wonder how we, or any country, could subject people to such soul-crushing circumstances as war.

In May of 1970 I received a call at Bangor Rivet shortly before I gave notice. It was from my father's "plain, little dumpling of a wife with the funny last name." She said, "Your father died last night in his sleep of a heart attack." I was struck numb and conflicted. He was only fifty-two. Hanging up, I told my boss. He suggested I leave work early. I trudged back home with my mind elsewhere. I barely even watched for traffic as I crossed the busy Route 135 intersection.

Back at my apartment I called and spoke with his wife again. This time I was babbling, going overboard. I was trying to be sympathetic and helpful, even saying, "If you don't want to stay where you are, I'll send you a plane ticket to go anyplace at all. If you wish, you can start over." I had no idea what was spilling out of my mouth. I had no idea how she was receiving it given her own emotional state. I was running on fumes. My brain was on auto-pilot.

Thankfully she did not take me up on my offer. There was no way I could have afforded to do it. My Aunt Rachel, who was visiting at that moment, and my mother were trying to get my attention, gesturing wildly, and shaking their heads "NO!" at me. Mindlessly, I did ask her to send a few things of his that were meaningful to me. There were some photos I wanted. I may have become a little overzealous and insensitive in my asking. She had her own immediate tragedy with which to contend. I don't know. I know I didn't mean to be insensitive.

Nothing happened. A month passed. I ended up asking her several times over the next month. She finally did send me send a few items of his in a way I never expected. They arrived by bus! This must have cost her. They were loose in a too-large carton with no packing material. Broken glass from the picture frames was everywhere. Glass shards had scratched and torn the photos. How could she have done this? We never spoke again. I almost regretted it. Except I thought what she had done was cruel. She could have safely sent me unframed photos in a large envelop. She could have done it for practically nothing by post.

As I later more fully recognized, thanks to K.H., I had *let* my father create this hole in me. I had done it inadvertently by *choosing* how I responded to my circumstances and to what he said and did. It really had been up to me not to let him do it to me. While I couldn't do anything at age seven, when I was a bit older, I could actually have acted in my own behalf. I could have distanced myself emotionally from him at any time. I could have ignored him. This was probably the best approach. I could have left and gone out on my own. This was less likely for me to do because of my concern for my mother.

There were options. I could have done a lot of things when I was older. But, by then I was hooked in. I didn't truly know I had those options. Or, if I knew I had them, I didn't know I could step back and pick the one option that would work best for me at that time. I discovered something else as well. Wallowing in my anger held something rewarding for me. Maybe I felt I needed to keep those negative feelings constantly raging within me. Maybe I needed the turmoil and pain to erase the numbness to make me feel I was still alive and in control. My K.H. lauded me for this awareness.

CHAPTER 34

Seeking Love, Deserving Pain

A day after my father's death, the father of a close college classmate died. Brian was at least twenty-five years older than my father and had lived a very active, productive life both socially and in business. He was well-known and well-respected in the Irish-American community. Despite my own grief, when his daughter, Rose, called me with the news, I immediately dropped everything. I went over to her home to personally comfort and support her.

Rose was eighteen years my senior, had lived in Framingham all her life, and had many friends as a result. When I arrived, I was all but lost in a sea of those friends and family. They crowded her mother's house giving condolences, sharing stories and nostalgia, eating, and drinking. After several hours of listening to Rose's grief, I begged off. I dragged myself home, even more depressed than when I'd left.

Brian's funeral was to be in a few days. I couldn't get out of my own way because of my father's death so I made a point of not committing myself to attending. I told her, "Please don't count on me to be there. My dad's death has hit me harder than I imagined it would." What added to my current despair was that despite Rose's having known about my father's death, she had never called to check on me. She never volunteered to see if *I* needed any comfort or support.

Ours had been a one-sided, inequitable relationship from the start. She would call me frequently to go over to her house. She would also request I bring my mother over to keep her elderly mother company. I imposed on my mother more than once—many more times than I should have—to do this. I regretted it each time.

My mother's reward was sitting with Rose's mother, Julia who spoke fractured English, watching television until Julia fell asleep. This always left my mother to find something to do before she gave me the high sign to go back home. I felt I was letting myself be treated like a doormat. Yet I didn't feel I could say "no" or stop it. By not doing anything about it, I was punishing myself again. I was getting what I deserved for being someone who was "unacceptable."

Rose was well-to-do as a result of working at a Boston television station and paying no housing expenses whatsoever because she lived with her parents. She traveled to Ireland with some frequency. From one trip she brought me back a silver pin for Christmas and from another, a small hand mirror. They were nice and thoughtful but I could never match them gift-wise.

Because of the paucity of my money, my gifts to her required my ingenuity and talents. Her level of disregard for me and my feelings became exquisitely evident one Christmas. It was the year I gave her a Romantic-style twenty-four by thirty-six-inch acrylic painting of two doves sitting together on a branch cooing to one another. I had done it especially for her. It had taken me over a week to complete it. When she unwrapped it, she looked disappointed.

I felt offended. But unlike my K.H., I didn't address it. Instead I acted as if I should apologize for my gift to her, "I wanted to do something a little different for you this year so I painted this since I know you like romantic things." Taking it, she scrutinized it then said somewhat dismissively, "You can always give me padded hangers."

Padded hangers? That's what I had done for her the year before. They were expensive. Anger engulfed me for my continuing to allow myself to take these ongoing insults. Why was I still tolerating this? Didn't I have any pride left at all?

I was unaware that I was "required" to attend Brian's funeral irrespective of my own father's death. When the day arrived, I definitely did not want to dress up for *them*, to go through all *their* rituals for *them* to share *their* grief, to console *them*, to be essentially invisible, a part of a large mass of mourners for *them*.

What I needed was time to myself to be in my own grief, and, maybe, be the object of someone else's sympathy. Hopefully, rolling my father's death around in my mind for a while with my K.H.'s help,

I could make some sense of my flooding feelings. Because of my not attending Brian's funeral, my life was about to play out the Law of Unintended Consequences. Whenever I did something purposefully, I got all kinds of unintended, unanticipated consequences along with what I expected and planned for. There's no way to know all the things that could or would happen as a result.

The day after Brian's service, my mother and I took a walk toward town. We had been making the best of the situation. I needed fresh air more than she since she had long since submerged her conflicts with him in as deep pool of roiling anger. She never forgave him for the long list of injuries he had inflicted on her. This was something that occasionally still boiled to the surface. Unlike me, she still reveled in her anger, allowing it to remain a large part of her for the rest of her life. I never wanted to live like that.

We stopped in a small pastry shop on Waverly that happened to be owned by one of Rose's older friends, Fiona. The moment we walked in, Fiona exploded, spewing venom all over me. In front of the five other people gathered there, she publicly castigated me for not having been at Brian's funeral.

"You didn't attend Brian's funeral! How could you do something so cruel to Rose? She expected you there. You were supposed to be her friend. You hurt her deeply. I can never forgive you for this and neither can Rose. Don't expect us to be friends any more. I don't want to see you or talk to you or even acknowledge you ever again." My K.H. would have stopped her flat with, "I didn't say I'd go to the funeral because my own father died. You can choose to accept that or not."

As if shocked by a live electrical wire by this out-of-the-blue onslaught, I stood silent, confused, and non-assertive. I was trying to gather my thoughts as her words slammed into me like rapid fire from an Uzi. I blushed and stammered. She superciliously waited for my reply. When I could regain the use of my tongue, I ventured to say something abysmally pathetic, "Maybe you didn't know my father had just died too—in Florida—I'm still trying to deal with that." Then somewhat helplessly I *even* asked for absolution by tossing in, "But I did go to see Rose when Brian died, before the funeral, to be there for her."

I was so outrageous I wanted to crawl away from myself. I took her unjustified criticism without a whimper when I should have stood up for myself. Fiona laughed derisively and spat at me. "You didn't even *like* your father!"

That verbal face slap was worse than any forsythia switch my father had used on my legs. It also shouted volumes about these people who had indicated they were my "friends." It made me ask myself: Why was Rose's grief more important than my grief? Did my driving over to emotionally support her mean nothing to her? Why didn't anyone show me any sympathy? And *only* my visibly attending a service with hundreds of others to acknowledge her father would have any meaning for her?

My K.H. shouted at the top of her lungs at me, "STOP IT! STOP IT THIS INSTANT! What's the matter with you? Her rant was so incredibly, irrationally brain-dead and you're responding to it as if it were rational. Good grief!" It hit me. I was asking rational questions about a totally irrational situation. I was again slipping into an analysis paralysis. I was acting like a slug, taking it all in and slithering away leaving an embarrassing slime trail behind. I had to do something about it.

I truly needed to change my course and do it now! That incident frightened me. If I didn't do something dramatic to reverse this downward slide of myself-worth, I would keep spiraling downward as my father had done. I couldn't let that happen. I had to undertake some immediate action.

Had we not happened to stop in Fiona's store, I would likely not have known for some time that I had been summarily expunged from Rose's list of "bosom buddies. No one ever made contact with me again in any way. BUT there was one very bright spot in all this. I *finally* realized how lucky I was to have been blackballed from their fold. I had known for a long time that I needed to extricate myself from my relationship with them. And now *they* had accommodatingly greased the skids. They had expedited the process for me. In spite of everything, I was grateful. I didn't know when I would have had the intestinal fortitude to have squirmed out from under their hobnail boots on my own. My K.H. reminded me, "Good for you."

As if the universe were trying to get my attention, something even stranger happened. The person I had been casually dating added to my recognition of my chronic case of "doormat-*itis*." Peter, a divorced clothing manufacturer's rep, who happened to be $10,000 in debt but was still spitting out money like an ATM on steroids, gave me an ultimatum. He told me unequivocally he didn't want to hear about my father's death.

In one breathe he had talked about his *never-to-be-realized* desire for us to *marry* (?) and in the next breath he told me as calmly as if he were ordering a chili dog with sauerkraut, "Look. I don't want to deal with your father's death. It's a bummer. It's your situation. It's your grief. You deal with it. You deal with it on your own. When you're done with the weeping, wailing, and gnashing of teeth, you can let me know. You can contact me because I won't contact you." That was another life lesson I would surely not forget. It was another reminder for me "to be careful whom I trust."

As my K.H. approved, I never got back in touch with him, even when he later tried through one of his pals to phone me. At that point, he retaliated by having one of his drinking buddies I barely knew ask me for a date and then never show up for it. That wasn't hard to figure out. Peter was the same person who told me when I had a painful vaginal infection, "If it's gonorrhea, I didn't give it to you and I won't pay for your medical treatment." What? Actually, I was thankful for his being so "sensitive" because it made me suddenly hyper-aware of what I had been doing to myself. I definitely had no intention of doing it any longer. These two incidents were painful but absolutely necessary eye-openers.

CHAPTER 35

Not Knowing What I Was

Awareness was not always easy or pleasant to access, even when I had my compassionate K.H. urging me on. It was becoming all too obvious that I had specifically picked Rose and Peter for intimates because I could sense how they'd treat me. They would not respect me. I had wanted two conflicting things from them. I wanted to be loved but I also wanted to be treated badly because I felt like I didn't deserve anything better. Finally the incandescent light bulb in my brain had been switched on. And now it would stay on.

I had to keep telling myself this stark truth. I was acting as if I were still that seven-year-old girl who wasn't wanted. I wasn't she any longer. I needed to move on. The pieces were sliding together into a pattern and gelling into something I could no longer ignore.

I had given up on getting into medical school—there were only single-digit openings for the hundreds of candidates who applied to each medical school. I had been away from my science studies for too long. I still needed more courses. Not surprisingly my father had always been against my becoming a physician. He seemed to exult in telling me, "The operating room is no place for a woman. They tell dirty jokes there. It's like a boys' club. You'd be really uncomfortable." I thought, but aren't most nurses in the operating room female? What's the difference? "Besides," he continued, "you should become a teacher and marry a salesman like me."

What he said made no sense but that was okay. If for some reason I couldn't be a physician, my father's male chauvinism aside, I'd find something else to accomplish. I could use my talents and satisfy those people-related needs and goals. I knew rationally there were lots of things I could do and do well. I had only to discover which ones would fit best where, and then follow them. Psychology seemed to be one solid possibility.

After I had received my first graduate degree in 1973 in English/Education, specializing in psychology, I worked as a consultant in interpersonal skills. Unlike most professionals, I had no idea how to handle the business end of it. Being a professional had no bearing whatsoever on being a good business person. That was a harsh, red-ink realization for me. I needed a mentor to clue me in. Without one, I slogged along until 1976. In 1976 I went for my second master's degree, this time in clinical psychology. At the same time I worked at Fairview State Hospital doing behavioral research. Since my goal was to go for my doctorate later on, I chose a non-terminal degree which emphasized research. Research was required for most psychology doctoral degrees unless one went for a degree at a "professional school." My mother, who was much stronger now, was ready to go out on her own. She decided to move to New Port Richey, Florida. She had friends from her days at the dress shop in Framingham who also had moved there. Enthusiastic about starting a new life, she was looking at her move as a new adventure.

We packed another U-Haul and hitched it to her car which I'd had a friend fix in the meantime so it was now reliable. Driving all the way to Florida, she and I moved her into a sunny two-bedroom apartment. It was replete with live ducks and squirrels on the lawn which would keep her company. She immediately found a job at the local hospital. Once she was settled in, I flew back.

Before I had finished the clinical program, Boston University had invited me to join their doctoral program in social psychology. I had planned to go into their clinical doctoral program but it was currently filled. Fortunately, B.U. at that time had an arrangement whereby I could obtain my Ph.D. in social psychology and then go through their clinical program as a post-doctoral student. That sounded like a feasible idea. Besides how people interacted with others and how it affected them really interested me and fit my work with interpersonal skills and social effectiveness. Because I worked on a teaching fellowship and then on research fellowship from the National Institutes of Mental Health, my Ph.D. program cost me next to nothing, except for books and supplies.

CHAPTER 36

Fearing Negative Evaluation

But all was not perfection quite yet. Despite my K.H., something most unexpected was stirring in me. It added to my lingering concerns about my "unacceptability." It was something that would change my future and not for the better in the short-term. At this time I admitted to myself I had been for at least a year feeling less comfortable socially. I had no understanding of the cause. I could still make small talk with classmates and instructors and give presentations in class. But now I was experiencing butterflies when I did it.

For some reason I was becoming unduly concerned about being negatively evaluated, found wanting, and perhaps rejected. I didn't know if it was coming only from my earlier experiences with my father's evaluation and rejection. Something else seemed to be insinuating itself into every aspect of my life as well. What self-confidence I had attained felt at risk. I was still doing well academically but knew I was socially vulnerable.

Whenever I could find Hepburn's films on television, I relished watching the real McCoy as she charged ahead with what she was tackling to achieve her goals. She was steadfastly going after what she desired. She was carving a path for herself through granite if necessary in order to acquire it. I, on the other hand, was finding myself slowly folding in on myself, becoming too introspective and emotionally self-involved. I was present but not as effectively active as I could be in achieving my personal goals. It seemed different from my being "unacceptable" but I didn't yet know how.

This inward turning progressed through my doctoral studies and into my post-doctoral training. I felt increasingly more insecure and anxious. However, when necessary, I could still, with effort, put on a mask of confidence and meet the "public." That was after I had gotten my loudly thumping heart, rapid, shallow breathing, and disconnection between my brain and my tongue under control to enable me to talk nearly intelligibly.

Not sure exactly what the problem was, I thought I was most likely suffering from Generalized Anxiety Disorder (GAD), wherein I would be anxious about everything in my life: health, finances, job, etc. I went to work on it with vigor, addressing it with cognitive and behavioral exercises. However, it didn't take long before I discovered that looking at my problem under that label was good but only as far as it went. Something important was missing.

Like an acrophobic looking into a dark hole, I was slowly being drawn into the void. I was falling into an abyss of paralyzing fear in any social interaction, or just the anticipation of it. Filled with an icy dread, I would sweat, tremble, and blush with strangers. I would expect terrible events to occur. In most situations I pushed through but suffered as I did. I "knew" everyone could probably see what was going on inside me. I felt humiliated as a result. In other social situations, I avoided or escaped whenever possible. I was becoming reclusive in many aspects of my life and constantly afraid.

In my worst moments I would freeze if the doorbell rang. I'd duck down if I were near a window or hide behind a door so no one could see I was home. The phone ringing petrified me. It was my mortal enemy because at that time there wasn't "caller ID." If I didn't know who was calling, I didn't know how I could respond to it. I didn't dare answer without a script because I knew I'd get tongue-tied and sound stupid.

I let the answering machine respond for me more times than not. But when I did, I would die a thousand fire-ant-stinging deaths if the person hung up without leaving a message. I was wrapped in worry that it might have been an important business call or client that I had missed. But still I couldn't bring myself to pick up the phone.

When my symptoms seemed at their isolation worse, I finally detected that everything about which I was anxious was related to *social* situations. That was like the heel of my hand slapping my forehead. Of course! That was my "aha!" It was at this juncture the *Diagnostic and Statistical Manual III,* the U.S. classification of clinical symptom descriptions of mental disorders for psychiatrists and psychologists, was finally talking in greater detail about "social anxiety disorder," also called "social phobia."

Now I knew what the missing piece to my anxiety puzzle was. I had to address my *social* symptoms specifically. I determined which situations were most anxiety-provoking then addressed them in a graduated, step-by-step manner. I positively reinforced every small success as I made my way up the steps. I knew how to do that. I read every clinical paper I could get my hands on the subject. I tailored my CBT, cognitive-behavioral therapy, to my social anxiety. And over time with lots of patience, persistence, and practice it worked and worked well!

As I unearthed what aided my overall recovery, I began to truly acknowledge the power of my K.H. and the real K.H. as the influential role model she provided. The more I observed and analyzed K.H., the more I knew what I needed to do. And the more I listened to my inner K.H., the more I began to blossom. Before me, within reach, was what I had been grasping for all my life. Both K.H.s represented my assertiveness, myself-esteem, self-confidence, self-respect, resilience, and ability to be tough when I needed to be.

I knew I was not alone in dealing with social anxiety. Some eighteen-to-twenty million people were likewise trying to cope and recover. Researching what was currently being done in various areas of treatment, I talked with the top clinical researchers in the field and with hundreds who suffered from this problem. There was a need for a self-help book to deal not only with the deep-seated anxiety itself but also with all the life skill strategies that had been lost during the anxiety's development.

As a social phobic trying to adapt to this overarching daily fear, I knew there was no room for concentrating on my K.H. Likewise, others would have difficulty seeing that their own inner voice held the key to making social skills possible. Without a K.H., achieving social effectiveness was a pipe dream. As a result, after my full recovery from my father *and* my social anxiety and two years of intensive research, I wrote *Diagonally-Parked in a Parallel Universe: Working Through Social Anxiety* to show others what I'd found that worked. Moreover, it showed how they could recover from social anxiety with the self-confidence and the social effectiveness they needed.

CHAPTER 37

Discovering the Roots of My Anxiety

Through this research I pinned down three critically important experiences that when they occur early in life can defeat healthy self-confidence and self-esteem. They can keep one deaf to a role model's coaching and help cause social anxiety.

The first factor is having overly critical parents. My father was the epitome of the overly critical parent. He was never quite satisfied with what I did. Rather than praise me for what I did right, he always pushed me to do better. But when I did do better, he re-adjusted the yardstick upward so that I could never quite reach his conception of "perfection" and acceptability. I was never to receive a gold star from him.

The second factor is having assertiveness-suppressing parents. My father also successfully suppressed any opinions, judgments, disagreements, questions, or assertiveness I had. This allowed me to doubt my own competence and confidence. I was not to stand up for myself no matter what. Standing up for myself in any manner was considered to be "disrespectful." "No" and "why" were forbidden. In taking away any self-expression and independence, he ignored my having any self-respect or true sense of self.

The third factor is having emotional insecurity. My father might as well have dropped me off at a state institution for all the emotional support he gave me as I was growing up. Although there were times that I suspected he might actually have been proud of my academic successes, he was loath to share it with me. This was likely because I was expected to do well. As his child, I represented him. I couldn't carry on his name to give him immortality, but when I did well, he could give himself credit. It was as if he, not I, were responsible for the success.

At the same time, I came to rarely glimpse the sensitive, hurting person within my father. This was a damaged soul who was still at war with his torturing captor father. He desperately wanted to break out and break free. Because his myriad fears and vulnerabilities had erected high, impenetrable walls around him, he couldn't or wouldn't even try to scale them to escape.

Unable to encourage me, he seemed to go out of his way to discourage me. He said I could "never succeed as a writer." My inner voice said that wasn't true. I reacted against that statement and made that untrue to prove the point. I wrote articles for national magazines, newspapers, and,initially, put out five non-fiction books. Irrespective of that, his assertion that I'd "never succeed as a writer" dampened my enthusiasm and efforts to pursue becoming a writer as an even larger part of my career.

Later on I had envisioned myself as a physician-writer, like Michael Crichton. When I was working at Scripps Clinic, Crichton visited to have their hematology department critique his *Andromeda Strain* for another book review. He was only one year older than I but already had fourteen published books under his belt. If I had only disabused myself of my father's "wisdom" earlier on, I wondered what I might possibly have accomplished with my writing.

In the same vein, he always said, "Your value as a person depends upon what you can earn in the marketplace." Despite its obvious irrationality, his "fact" had a lingering effect on me for both good and ill. I continued to hear it ricocheting in my mind throughout the decades. However, I labored to fight against it. That was his reality, his definition, not mine.

To show him, and me, in my mind it wasn't true, I made a point of volunteering. I contributed to people in need, rescued animals, cooked for the homeless, and fought for environmental causes and against all types of social injustice. These were all activities that were *guaranteed* not to make me any money. Instead, they made me feel good. They also, hopefully, produced positive results of which I could be proud. Still in the back of my head I wondered if I *could* make the kind of money to which he alluded. If I could have, would it have given me that special "value as a person" status he so prized? I was unlikely to know as I wasn't interested in trying to do so.

Ironically, by his own definition, my father would have had no "value as a person." That was something of which I'm sure he was aware. He only intermittently held a job, made some money, lost it, and never truly supported his family. He would have been considered a "failure" in the marketplace. Perhaps this was because all his life he too had contended with an overly critical, assertiveness suppressing, emotional-insecurity-inducing parent—his own father. But he couldn't rise above it.

His early life had left him angry, frustrated, depressed, and ultimately dysfunctional. He was unable to see that he could actually effect some kind of positive change for himself in his life. He didn't have to feel like a failure but he did because he allowed his father to actively help keep him feeling that way.

CHAPTER 38

Forgiving My Father

As a result, he unconsciously passed that lethal legacy on down to his children. Becoming aware of this, I purposely worked to step back to see my father from a different perspective. I needed to see him as he really was: an individual who had an unfortunate history that left him disabled and suffering. He was one who was truly struggling to exist as a person with any sense of self. But within the strict confines of his father-dominated life he couldn't achieve it his "self." He was so caught up in his own emotional turmoil that he could not see beyond himself, much less extend himself to others in any meaningful way.

He couldn't be there for any of us because he could barely be there for himself. Fear, anger, and disappointment ruled then conquered his life. I'm sure the resulting hollowness of his soul felt irreversible without the awareness he needed. In order to reverse it, he would have had to be open to his own buried inner voice, acknowledge his situation, work at it, and be open to painful change. He would have had to believe it was possible to change, to see not only that there could be something better but also that he could gain it.

Sadly, my father's problem seemed to be cemented in his psyche. He couldn't let go of his negative emotion and his feeling like a super-victim of his father, wife, family, and of his existence in general. It became his identity and his method of operating in life. It led him to become increasingly self-centered about his pain and loss.

For him to share love, compassion, empathy, or even a little caring was tantamount to taking it away from his own finite resource of them. The more he shared, the less there would be for him until he would reach depletion. That was a risk he could not afford to take. He already had so little and needed so much more just to survive, much less start to fill that hole in his soul.

In the end he had lost his ability to objectively see what was going on and rationally address it. His life in his father's shadow had produced an individual who was merely a shade of who he might have been. He was simply unequipped to analyze these situations, list reasonable options, make considered decisions, and then act practically on them. Like me *before* my recovery, my father kept waiting for the unpredictable yet inevitable newspaper to swat him, causing him intractable emotional distress.

He learned to fear his father as he simultaneously longed to love him and be loved back. My father was, in fact, an older generation's version of "me" *if* I had not stepped up to the plate, swung at the ball, made contact, and run around the bases. It was a stark realization I took to heart.

I think now that my keeping in touch with him was the right thing to do. I had to forgive my father because he wasn't a bad person. He was a sad person whose presence in the lives of others constantly created problems. He was like cartoonist Al Capp's hapless "Joe Btfsplk," the world's worst jinx who brought disastrous misfortune to everyone around him. Perpetually hovering above his head was a dark rain cloud. The only difference between "Joe" and my father was that my father's dark rain cloud hovered inside of him, distorting the size and shape of his heart.

And, just maybe, if he had had the opportunity to live longer, my father *might* have been able to claw his way out of that self-imposed manure pit. With some help he might have been able to come to terms with himself and gain some insight from it. To paraphrase "High Flight's" 19-year-old pilot and poet, John Gillespie Magee, Jr., maybe he could have "slipped the surly bonds of history to touch the face of awareness."

However, in all honesty I have to doubt it would have occurred. Not recognizing his own inner voice, he had accommodated to his vampire-controlled lot in life. It was very likely he would have felt that the devil you know is better than the devil you don't know. Change was risky. At least he knew what to expect. It was awful but he could predict and control it in his own way. There was some comfort in that, despite the pain and anger.

CHAPTER 39

Empowering Myself!

My life with my father was an education I would have preferred to have acquired in some other way. It did, however, leave me with some valuable lessons.

I learned that my K.H. was like a rational coach sitting on my right shoulder, guiding me objectively, cheering me on against the irrational vampire sitting on my left shoulder. The vampire was all the negative emotional garbage that I had absorbed from others and had unconsciously allowed to rule and direct me. It tried to consume all my life essence.

As I listened to and followed my coach, I recognized how the vampire affected me. I disengaged from its negative emotion. I cast aside my "doormat" status so as to let my independence and self-confidence bloom. As my coach became larger, the vampire became smaller, and smaller, finally disappearing in a puff of sunlight-induced smoke.

I learned that everyone has their own inner coach to which to listen. My K.H. inner coach showed me how I could stand up for myself, my rights, and my principles. My K.H. helped me develop my personhood, choose my goals, and reach my potential.

I learned that I had to see my parents—and others who had hurt me—outside their role in relation to me. I needed to see them as individuals with their own checkered history. They too had experienced hurtful situations and struggled with distressing problems—problems with which they were likely still wrestling internally, just like me. I had to forgive them and I did forgive them.

When I forgave my father for his emotional abuse, I experienced the intoxication of knowing that I could walk away from him feeling good, whole, redeemed, and guilt-free. I had shed my internalized struggle with him like a snake skin. I now knew no one could make me feel bad about myself without my consent. That is a feeling of incredible lightness like no other. I blew all my hurtful early experiences—and their lingering negative emotions—into a balloon, securely tied it, and let it go to fly away on the winds to vanish in the jet stream.

What this means is that in spite of my father—but also strangely because of him—I have accomplished a great deal of what I have wanted most in my life. I used his attitudes and behavior to force me to look hard within myself to seek resources and strength I didn't know I had. When I was seven years old, it felt like a sink or swim situation. I did whatever I thought I had to in order to survive. But as I grew older, more rational, and aware, I could see there were options available to me. I could purposely choose what was most likely to help me achieve each of my goals.

Once I started listening to my inner voice and assigned a strong role model to it, I figured out who I wanted to be as a person. Because my parents were individually and collectively dysfunctional, they were sadly incapable of performing their roles effectively. Consequently, *I had to become my own parent,* though I didn't know it as a child. Desperately seeking nurturing, I came to learn to nurture not only myself but also others. I also discovered during this journey to recovery that the more I gave to others in love and friendship the more I had available to give. And the more I received in return. It was the same with strength, resilience, and courage in confronting challenges. In forgiving my father, I forgave myself as well. This was something I desperately needed to do and fully deserved to do.

The following sum up a lot of what I've experienced to become "acceptable":

"Opportunities to find deeper powers within ourselves come when life seems most challenging." — Joseph Campbell

"You gain strength, courage, and confidence with every experience in which you really stop to look fear in the face. You are able to say to yourself I have lived through this horror. I can take the next thing that comes along. You must do the thing you think you cannot do." – Eleanor Roosevelt

"Each one has to find his peace from within. And peace to be real must be unaffected by outside circumstances." – Mohandas Gandhi

Ultimately, I was the one who gave myself permission to be *unconditionally acceptable*. This means I am acceptable irrespective of what anyone else might think, say, or do. The result of being *unconditionally acceptable* is feeling good in my own skin. It is feeling free to do what I want the way I want to do it. I became the strong, productive individual I wanted to be and did it—mostly—my way. Perhaps it isn't so surprising then that I became a psychologist-coach, animal rescuer, kitty mom, and author.

Finally, I learned that "growing up 'unacceptable'" does *not* have to be a life sentence or a catastrophic disaster. It can be merely a small bump in the road. With the help of my inner "Katharine Hepburn," I rescued myself! Now I can gloriously kick-butt.

ABOUT THE AUTHOR

Signe A. Dayhoff, PhD, is a social psychologist with post-graduate training in counseling, positive psychology, and emotional intelligence who received her doctorate from Boston University. There she studied interpersonal communication skills, social effectiveness, personal marketing. and use of mentors. For over 30 years she has been a coach, educator, and author, specializing in social anxiety, self-confidence, and self-presentation.

She is a certified Authentic Happiness Coach and administer/interpreter of the *Mayer-Salovey-Caruso Emotional Intelligence Test,* has taught psychology at Boston University, University of Massachusetts, and Framingham State College, and has done research at Massachusetts Institute of Technology, Scripps Clinic and Research Foundation, and Fairview State Hospital.

Author of 17 books, including the 2nd Ed. of *Diagonally-Parked in a Parallel Universe: Working Through Social Anxiety* (2010), the social phobic's bible and insider's scoop on social effectiveness strategies, she has contributed to David Riklan's *101 Great Ways to Improve Your Life (Vol. 2)* and Steven J. Bennett's *Executive Chess: Creative Problem Solving By 45 of America's Top Business Leaders and Thinkers.* EffectivenessPlus.com. She is also an applied feline behaviorist, animal rescuer, and "kitty mom" to 20-plus elderly cats, who consults and speaks on human-cat bond, cat communication, and human-cat relationships.

www.ingramcontent.com/pod-product-compliance
Lightning Source LLC
Chambersburg PA
CBHW071959040426

42447CB00009B/1401